food to go

Packed lunches, light meals, after sport
snacks, weekend treats & much more...

PUBLISHED BY:
Hyndman Publishing,
P O Box 5017, Dunedin

ISBN:
1-877382-01-9

TEXT:
© Simon & Alison Holst

PHOTOGRAPHY:
© Hyndman Publishing,
except pages 6, 25
and 53 © New Holland
Publishers (NZ) Ltd.

DESIGN:
Dileva Design Ltd.

PHOTOGRAPHY:
Lindsay Keats

FOOD STYLING:
Simon and Alison Holst

Important Information:

For best results, use a standard metric (250ml) measuring cup and metric measuring spoons when you use these recipes.

1 tablespoon holds 15ml.
1 teaspoon holds 5ml.

All the cup and spoon measures in the recipes are level, unless otherwise stated. Sets of measuring cups make it easier to measure ¼ and ½ cup quantities.

Larger amounts of butter are given by weight. Use pack markings as a guide. Small amounts of butter are measured using spoons (1 tablespoon of butter weighs about 15 grams).

Abbreviations used:

ml	millilitre
tsp	teaspoon
Tbsp	tablespoon
g	gram
°C	Celsius
cm	centimetre

Acknowledgements:

We would like to thank the following firms:

- **Alison's Choice:** for high quality dried fruit, fruit mixtures, crystallised fruit, nuts, seeds, cornmeal, chocolate chips and morsels which were used in all recipe development and photographs.
- **Benniks Poultry Farm**, Buller Road, Levin: RSPCA approved barn-laid eggs.
- **William Aitken:** for Lupi oils, grapeseed oil, and Balsamic vinegar.

For more information on these (and other titles) visit www.hyndman.co.nz or **www.holst.co.nz**

Contents

Introduction

We think that "food to go" should be easy, interesting, varied and fun!

Although packed weekday lunches are probably the first thing you think of as "food to go", we hope that you will find the ideas in this book are suitable for many other situations too!

- What about a weekend picnic?
- Feel like an impromptu after-work, summery family meal at a nearby park or playground?
- Need to get the kids out of the house during school holidays?
- Been to the zoo lately, with a packed lunch in a backpack?
- What about ringing family friends and suggesting you eat a casual meal together, at your house or theirs, and watch a good DVD?
- Want something warm and fortifying to enjoy before, during or after a match on a cold wintry day?
- Know somewhere with a view, where you can enjoy a light meal in, or close to the car?
- Do you feel housebound and in need of a "breath of fresh air"?
- Is a mini-celebration called for? Good marks at school? Unexpected good news? Or, perhaps just a little treat for someone special? Take your meal (and a bottle of wine) somewhere different!

We are sure that you will think of many other times when it would be so much more fun to "grab something easy and go" rather than sitting round the table at home.

Flip through these pages until you find something that appeals, and suits your particular situation. Remember that food doesn't need to be complicated or unduly costly to please everybody.

Not every recipe will suit all situations. Some of our ideas are for making at home, before you go out. Others require a microwave oven, a grill or toaster oven of some type for reheating or browning, or perhaps the use of a portable barbecue. Some may be heated before you leave home, then carried in a thermos.

AND last but not least, we want you to know that we have nothing against sandwiches, as you will realise when you read our sandwich suggestions! We do hope though, that this book will encourage you to try something a little different, to be adventurous with your/our "food to go", and really enjoy it.

Simon & Alison Holst

Pick and go

In a perfect world, we would all have time to assemble our perfect tasty (and preferably healthy) lunch to take with us before heading out the door to work, school or just to play, in the morning! Unfortunately, all of us have days where this just doesn't happen.

While there is a whole industry ready to cater to your lunchtime needs (cafés, lunch bars, tuck shops and assorted other fast food and takeaway outlets), if you can get to a supermarket there are many options that are probably easier on the wallet (and quite probably the waistline!) These fall into two basic categories.

There are those which you can keep 'on hand' in your desk drawer or locker for a week or so, bringing them out when necessary on those days when you just can't get away, even for a few minutes. Or second, are those which you can pop into a store to buy on the day you want to eat them.

Foods to keep 'on hand':

- **Good quality "bulk" or "self-selection" dried fruits**, preferably in resealable plastic bags. There is a wonderful range to choose from, and they are good for you, so keep several different varieties on hand. Try mixtures of chopped fruits too.
- **"Self-selection" nuts**, single varieties or mixtures, again best in resealable bags. Nuts have definite health benefits and a small handful a day is recommended. Again, don't just stick with one variety!
- **Fruit leathers**
- **Little tins of tuna or salmon** – go for cans with pull tabs or keep a good can opener in your drawer too. If you want to eat them "straight" choose those flavoured, in sauce, etc. Good with crackers or rice cakes which also keep well.
- **Crackers, crisp breads, rice cakes, bread sticks etc.**
- **Small plastic pottles (or tins) of fruit or fruit purée mixtures**
- **Long-life milk or soy milks**, plain or flavoured
- **Muesli or other cereals**, in small cartons or from "bulk" food departments. Eat dry, with yoghurt, fruit juice, milk from the tea-room or from small cartons mentioned above, maybe with a sliced banana.
- **Little packs of plain or spreadable cheese with crackers**, or packets of small crackers
- **"Self-selection" pretzels, snippets, peanut butter pretzels** to eat alone or with dips or spreads.
- **Muesli or energy bars**
- **Sweet Biscuits** (not such a healthy option perhaps, but there is now quite a variety of large, individually wrapped biscuits to choose from).
- **Instant soups** (powdered sachets, heat and eat pouches etc.)
- **Fresh fruits** – some fresh fruits, particularly oranges, mandarins and bananas will keep on hand for a few days.
- **Baked beans & spaghetti** – now come in small, tear-top cans. Whack them in a bowl and zap in the microwave for a minute or so!
- **Instant rice and noodle pottles** – these aren't as good as the 'real thing', but they're better than nothing, very easy, and do keep well!

Foods to grab and eat on the day (any of the above plus):

- **Fresh fruit and vegetables** – apples, oranges, grapes, kiwifruit, tomatoes – there's a whole produce department to choose from!
- **Bread rolls** – many 'in-store' bakeries sell individual rolls (very cheaply), grab one or two, then head to the deli for your choice of fillings.
- **Deli delights** – another whole department to choose from – you really can pick up an entire picnic here! Ham, salami, smoked salmon and other cured meats, surimi, olives, sundried tomatoes, chargrilled capsicums, salads etc, all in quantities to suit you.
- **Little pots of puddings**
- **Pottles of yoghurt, cottage cheese etc.**
- **Little individually wrapped cheeses**
- **Hummus, pâtés and dips from the chiller**

We're sure this is by no means a complete and comprehensive list, but hopefully it will provide some food for thought on those bad days!

Liquid Lunches
(Soups and Smoothies)

In cooler weather, what could be more welcome at lunchtime than home-made soup? It's perfect to prepare in advance, then carry to work in a Thermos or other container to reheat in the lunchroom microwave. Enjoy it too, steaming from a Thermos, on the sideline before, during or after the 'big game', or just sitting round the table for a hearty weekend lunch.

Minestrone

The list of ingredients may look fairly long, but minestrone is really quite simple to make. It is a substantial soup and makes a delicious lunch alone or with crusty bread.

For 6–8 servings:

1 Tbsp olive oil
1–2 rashers bacon
(optional)
2 cloves garlic
1 large onion, diced
4 cups chicken or
vegetable stock
2 medium carrots
2 medium sticks celery
1 medium potato
425g can kidney beans
400g can whole tomatoes
in juice
¾ cup small pasta shapes
1 cup frozen peas
2 cups sliced cabbage
2 Tbsp chopped parsley
2 Tbsp pesto or ¼ cup
chopped basil (optional)
½ tsp each dried oregano
and thyme
1 tsp salt
freshly ground black
pepper
grated Parmesan cheese
and pesto to serve

Heat the oil in a large pot over a medium heat. Chop the bacon (if using) and cook until golden, then add the chopped garlic and onion. Cook, stirring occasionally, for 5 minutes or until the onion is soft and clear.

Stir in stock, then add the finely diced fresh vegetables. Add the drained and rinsed beans, then the canned tomatoes, breaking them up with a fork. Bring the soup to the boil, then reduce the heat, cover and simmer for 30 minutes or until the potato is tender.

Add the pasta, peas, cabbage, herbs and seasonings. Simmer for 10–15 minutes or until the pasta is tender but still firm. Check the seasoning and add some water if you think the soup is too thick.

Serve immediately, or divide into serving sized portions and refrigerate or freeze to take to work and reheat as required, or to put in a Thermos.

NOTE: For vegetarian soup, omit the bacon and use vegetable rather than chicken stock.

Use your own homemade stock, or ready to use bought stock from tetrapaks or pouches, or, make up 'Instant' stock from powders or concentrates (usually 1 tsp per cup of water.)

Corn & Ham Chowder

A big bowl of this thick, creamy soup, packed with corn, other vegetables and ham, makes a satisfying lunch (or even dinner) on a cold day. While it's quick enough to make for immediate consumption, it can also be made ahead and packed in a Thermos for a warming lunch at work (or refrigerate it and microwave when required).

For 4 large servings:

1 Tbsp oil
25g butter
1 glove garlic, minced
1 large onion, finely diced
1 medium carrot, finely diced
2 tender celery stalks, thinly sliced (optional)
2 medium–large potatoes, finely diced (about 300g)
2 cups hot water
2 tsp instant chicken stock
2 Tbsp cornflour
2 cups milk
440g can cream-style corn
100–200g diced ham
2 tsp basil pesto (optional)
salt and pepper to taste
chopped parsley and/or chives

Place a large pot over a moderate heat, then add the oil and butter. When the butter has melted stir in the garlic and onion. Cook stirring frequently until the onion has softened, then add the remaining vegetables and cook for 3–4 minutes longer, stirring frequently to prevent browning. Add the hot water and instant stock, then cover and simmer gently until the vegetables are cooked through.

Mix the cornflour to a paste with about ¼ cup of the milk. When the vegetables are tender, add the remaining milk to the pot, then stir in the cornflour paste. Allow the mixture to come to the boil, stirring occasionally, then add the creamed corn, ham and pesto (if using). Mix thoroughly and simmer for 5–10 minutes.

Season to taste with salt and pepper (you may not need any salt, depending on the saltiness of the ham), and add the herbs.

Serve in large bowls with (warmed) crusty bread or rolls.

Alphabet Soup

This popular soup is so quick to make, you can whip it up anytime you get the urge, or even make a batch before going off to work in the morning (pack it in a Thermos or reheat it in the microwave).

For 4 servings:

4 cups of chicken stock
1 tsp sugar
2 tsp butter
3 Tbsp alphabet noodles (or up to ½ cup larger pasta)
1 small onion, peeled and finely chopped
1 stick celery, thinly sliced
1 small carrot, grated
1 small potato, grated
1 tomato, diced
1 Tbsp chopped parsley
salt and pepper to taste

Put the stock in a medium sized saucepan over high heat. Add the sugar and butter. When this mixture comes to the boil add the noodles.

Prepare and add the vegetables in the given order. Chop the onion and celery, grate the carrot and scrubbed potato and chop the tomato. The soup should be cooked about 10–15 minutes (depending on the size of pasta used) after the noodles are added.

Stir in the chopped parsley and season to taste with salt and pepper. Serve immediately, or cool and reheat later.

NOTE: If you can find them, pasta "alphabets" are a handy and fun little shape for soups, but of course you can use any other pasta shapes too. Vermicelli or thin egg noodles are good for people who enjoy sucking up long thin shapes (not so good at work!), while bigger shapes give the soup a very substantial feel.

Chorizo & Bean Soup

It is hard to believe this satisfying and substantial soup can be prepared in just 20 minutes or so!

For 4–6 servings:
2 Tbsp olive or canola oil
1 medium–large onion,
   peeled and diced
2 cloves garlic, minced
1 medium potato
1 medium carrot, scrubbed
2 sticks celery, thinly sliced
200g chorizo sausages,
   thinly sliced
2 x 400g cans cannellini
   beans
4 cups chicken stock
½ tsp dried thyme
½ tsp dried basil
½–1 tsp salt
pepper to taste
3–4 Tbsp chopped parsley

Heat the oil in a large pot. Add the onion and garlic and cook, stirring frequently to prevent browning, until the onion has softened. While the onion cooks, finely dice the scrubbed but unpeeled potato and carrot (the smaller the dice, the faster they will cook). Stir these into the pot along with the celery and chorizo and continue to cook, stirring frequently, for three to four minutes longer, until the chorizo begins to brown.

Rinse and drain the beans, then add them with the stock, then sprinkle in the basil and thyme. Bring the mixture to the boil, then reduce the heat to a simmer and cook for 10–15 minutes, stirring occasionally.

Taste the soup and season with salt and pepper. (The quantity of salt required will depend on how salty the chorizo are). Stir in most of the parsley, reserving a little to use as a garnish, and cook for a few minutes longer before serving.

Delicious as it is, or add some crusty bread and a side salad to turn this into a complete and satisfying meal.

Thai-style Pumpkin Soup

Good old pumpkin soup with a twist! The addition of some Asian seasonings breathes new life into this old favourite. If you're wondering why add the carrot and kumara to pumpkin soup, it's because the carrot adds some extra sweetness, while the kumara seems to give an extra silky smoothness.

For 10 cups, about 8 servings:
2 Tbsp olive oil
1 large or 2 medium onions
2 tsp red or green curry
   paste
4 cups chicken stock
2 medium carrots
1kg peeled and seeded
   pumpkin
2 medium kumara
400ml can coconut cream*
2 Tbsp fish sauce
fresh coriander to garnish
   (optional)

*use 'lite' coconut cream if desired

Heat the oil in a large pot, add the finely chopped onion and cook until the onion is transparent but has not browned. Add the curry paste and cook for 2–3 minutes longer, stirring often, before adding the chicken stock.

Prepare the vegetables by peeling and cutting them into cubes. Add to the pot as each is prepared, starting with the carrots first, since these require a little longer cooking than the pumpkin or kumara. Cook for 10–12 minutes or until the vegetables are tender. For best flavour and colour, do not cook longer than necessary.

Blend or process in batches, then pour through a sieve back into a clean pot. Add the coconut cream and fish sauce, and bring back to the boil. Adjust seasonings if necessary.

Serve immediately or refrigerate or freeze and reheat when required. A garnish of fresh coriander leaves is a nice touch, if available.

Chicken Laksa

When we get to 'hit the food halls' we both love large, steaming bowls of laksa (a creamy, curried noodle soup). Fortunately, since you don't always have a food hall handy, you can quite easily make your own!

For 2–3 servings:
2 Tbsp curry powder
3 Tbsp blanched almonds
  or cashew nuts
2–3cm piece fresh ginger,
  peeled
2 cloves garlic, peeled
1–2 tsp Thai red curry
  paste (optional)
1 lemon or lime, zest and
  juice
2 Tbsp water
2 Tbsp canola oil
3 cups chicken stock
¾ cup coconut cream
1 Tbsp fish sauce
300g boneless, skinless
  chicken breast or thighs
1 medium–large carrot, cut
  into match sticks
100g baby spinach leaves,
  Asian greens or green
  beans
400g fresh egg noodles*
100g bean sprouts
chopped fresh coriander
  and/or spring onion to
  garnish

Combine the first seven ingredients in a blender or food processor (or mortar and pestle) and process (or pound) to make a smooth paste.

Heat the oil in a large pot, then add the paste and cook, stirring continuously for 1 minute. Stir in the stock, coconut cream and fish sauce, then heat until boiling.

While the soup comes to the boil, cut the chicken into thin strips or 1cm cubes. Drop the prepared chicken, carrot and green vegetables into the soup and simmer for 4–5 minutes until the chicken is cooked through.

During this time place the noodles in a large sieve and rinse them with boiling or very hot water to soften, then divide them between serving bowls.

Ladle the soup into the bowls trying to divide the chicken and vegetables evenly between each. Garnish with a few bean sprouts, some chopped coriander and/or sliced spring onion and serve immediately.

*If you can't buy fresh egg noodles you can use the instant long life (vacuum packed) ones, or they can be replaced with rice sticks (available from larger supermarkets and Asian food stores). Simply soak 200g of thick rice sticks in boiling water for 5 minutes then divide them between the bowls.

"Meal in a Bowl" Soup ▼

This soup for one is a real treat! It has a wonderful flavour, is a complete (low fat) meal (lunch or dinner), and can be prepared and cooked in less than 10 minutes.

For speed and convenience we use precooked rice or pasta – you can use leftovers or use the instant vacuum packed varieties you can buy in the supermarket.

For 1 large (main) serving:

- 75g boneless, skinless salmon or other fish or about 75g cooked chicken
- 1 large or 2 small spring onions
- 1 cup cooked brown or white rice or 1 cup cooked small pasta shapes
- 1½ cups homemade or bought chicken stock
- ½ tsp grated fresh root ginger, optional
- 1 tsp Kikkoman soya sauce
- 1 tsp sesame oil
- 1 tsp Thai sweet chilli sauce, optional
- 2 Tbsp chopped fresh coriander leaves, basil, parsley or other herbs
- 4–6 button mushrooms
- ¼–½ ripe avocado, optional
- salt and pepper to taste

Cut the raw salmon or other fish into 1cm cubes, or cut the cooked chicken into chunky but manageable pieces. Slice spring onions about 5mm thick, diagonally. Cut the mushrooms and avocado into pieces about the same size as the fish.

Put all the ingredients except the salt and pepper in a large, microwavable, fairly deep soup bowl or in a medium-sized pot.

Microwave the bowl of ingredients for about 5 minutes, until it is very hot but has not boiled. (The fish will cook in this time.) Or bring all the ingredients in the pot to the boil and simmer gently for 5 minutes. Season and serve immediately.

Smoothies

These smoothies have delicious fresh flavours, contain virtually no fat and yet are high in calcium, fibre and other 'goodies' (including 1.5–2 servings of fruit per serving). They're more substantial than you'd expect and make an excellent almost instant light meal on the run.

There are really very few 'hard and fast' rules to smoothie making – you can use many different combinations of fruit (try using cubed fresh pineapple, sliced mango, peaches, nectarines, strawberries, raspberries or gold kiwifruit – or combinations of these – in place of the fruits suggested below).

If you want some extra flavour variations, try adding a teaspoon of vanilla essence and/or for something really different a little grated fresh ginger really gives things a lift! Alternatively, for something more decadent, you can use icecream in place of yoghurt.

Blueberry & Banana Smoothie

The berries give this an amazing colour.

For 2 large servings:
1 medium banana
1 cup frozen (or fresh) blueberries
½ cup plain or fruit flavoured low fat yoghurt
3 household dessertspoons of honey
1 cup calcitrim (or other reduced fat) milk

Break the peeled banana into 3–4 pieces and place in a blender or food processor with blueberries, yoghurt, and honey. Process until smooth.

Add the milk to the blender or processor and whiz again just enough to make a thick smooth drink (try to avoid blending/processing for too long or you will crush up the blueberry seeds making the drink gritty).

Pour into glasses and enjoy!

Zippy Zespri Smoothie

A little fresh ginger makes this really refreshing!

For 2 large servings:
1 medium banana
4 ice cubes (optional)
½ cup plain, unsweetened low fat yoghurt
2–3 household dessertspoons of honey
3 medium green kiwifruit
1 cup reduced fat milk
1–2 tsp finely grated ginger

Break the peeled banana into a blender or food processor. Add the ice cubes (if using), yoghurt and honey. Process until smooth.

Thinly peel the kiwifruit, then cut into quarters or chunks and add to the blender or processor with the milk and ginger. Whiz again just enough to make a thick smooth drink (don't blend/process for too long after you've added the kiwifruit or you will crush up the seeds making the drink unpleasantly gritty).

Pour into two tall glasses and enjoy!

Use Your Loaf

(Sandwiches, Rolls and more)

We once read somewhere that 70% of all the meals 'cooked' at home in the US were 'sandwiches'.
At first this seemed both incredible (and more than a little alarming!), but upon further reflection it
begins to make a little more sense – they're not talking about a vegemite or peanut butter sandwich.
All sorts of huge and complicated filled rolls (hoagies, subs, etc) and even hamburgers were
probably included – if it's in bread, it's a sandwich. We've taken
something of this approach here.

Barbecued Flank Steak Sandwiches

This is very much in the American school of sandwiches – it's not just something you knock up on the spur of the moment, but when it is completed it does make a substantial meal for 3–4 adults.

For 4 servings:
1 medium red onion (for marinade)
2 cloves garlic
¼ cup lemon juice
2 Tbsp soy sauce
2 tsp sesame oil
about 600g flank steak (in one piece)
1 medium onion, peeled and sliced (for filling)
1 Tbsp olive or canola oil
2–3 Tbsp mayonnaise
2–3 Tbsp Dijon mustard
1 French stick
lettuce or mesclun
tomatoes

Peel and quarter the onion. Place in a food processor or blender along with the next four ingredients and process until you have a smoothish paste.

Lie the steak on a board. Using a sharp knife, lightly score the surface in a diamond pattern. Turn it over and do the same on the other side. Place the steak in a large (unpunctured) plastic bag and pour in the onion marinade. Massage the bag so both sides of the steak are well covered with the paste, then squeeze out as much air as possible from the bag and leave to marinate for at least 15 minutes.

To cook, preheat a grill plate (or large, heavy frypan) on a barbecue or stove over a high heat. Remove the steak from the bag and gently shake off excess marinade. Lightly non-stick spray the grill plate (or pan) and add the steak. Cook for 3 minutes per side (skirt steak needs to be rare or it will be tough), then remove from the heat and set aside for about 5 minutes.

While the steak rests, cook the onion in the oil until soft and beginning to brown, and mix the mustard and mayonnaise together.

To serve, thinly slice the steak across the grain with the knife held at 45° to the board. Split the French stick and spread both sides with the mustard-mayonnaise mixture. Add some lettuce or mesclun, some sliced tomatoes, a layer of the fried onion and a generous layer of the beef. Replace the top of the loaf and serve.

Tuna Salad Roll

We frequently make variants of this easy salad for weekday lunches – just grab a can of tuna from the pantry and grab a few odds and ends from the fridge and you're ready to eat in a couple of minutes.

For 3–4 servings as a 'sandwich' filling:
220g can tuna in water or brine, drained
1 Tbsp lemon juice
2–3 Tbsp mayonnaise
2 medium-sized ripe tomatoes
about 10cm cucumber
2 sticks celery
2–3 Tbsp chopped parsley
salt and pepper to taste

Tip the tuna into a medium sized bowl, add the lemon juice and mayonnaise and stir until combined and the tuna is broken up.

Cut the tomatoes and cucumber into small dice, and thinly slice or dice the celery, then stir the vegetables and parsley into the tuna mixture. Season to taste with salt and pepper and you're ready to go.

If you're in a low-carb mood, enjoy as it is (it will serve two or three like this) or if you want something a little more portable it makes a great sandwich or roll filling, especially if you add a little lettuce or a handful of mesclun and possibly a slice or two of tomato.

'Basic' Sandwiches

For variety and fun, we use the term "sandwich" loosely! Think outside the square and don't limit yourself to conventional sliced bread. Experiment with breads. Remember that the bread alone, especially wholegrain and wholemeal varieties, make sandwiches a nutritionally worthwhile as well as convenient option.

Wrap, roll, fill, fold or stuff various breads using some of the fillings from the following lists. Enjoy the variety available! Look carefully in supermarkets and bakeries. Keep your eyes open for new products – and don't forget home-made breads if you make your own bread.

Thin sliced bread	Bread and dinner rolls	Foccacia	Muffins
Thick sliced bread	Baps	Ciabatta	English muffins
White bread	Hamburger buns	Turkish loaves	Bagels
White (high fibre) bread	Long (hot-dog) buns	Mountain breads	Croissants
Wholemeal bread	Currant buns	Lavash	Rice cakes
Fruit breads	French bread	Pizza breads	Pikelets
Multigrain bread	Pita/pocket breads	Flour tortillas	Crêpes
Heavy multigrain bread	Panini	Naan breads	Pancakes

Wraps and Roll-ups

Large flat breads make wonderful wraps and roll-ups. Spread them with cream cheese, mayonnaise or leftover satay sauce, shredded lettuce or cabbage, grated carrot and cheese. Add a little cooked chicken, shaved ham, last night's leftovers etc, for variety. Roll up firmly, and cut in manageable lengths. Keep cool until required (refrigerate or store in insulated containers, which now come lunch box sized).

Butter and Margarine Spreads

No one likes a sandwich that falls apart, but many "sandwiches" don't need butter or margarine to hold them together. Don't use high fat spreads from force of habit, especially with fillings containing peanut butter, cream cheese, mayonnaise etc. If you want them, or when they are necessary, use easy-to-spread products sparingly and look for salt and fat reduced varieties.

Individual Sandwich Fillings

There's more to sandwich fillings than marmite, cheese and peanut butter! The fillings can be used singly – although of course not all will suit all tastes. (Mixed fillings follow.)

Asparagus, freshly cooked or canned	Cottage cheese, plain or flavoured
Avocado slices (with lemon juice)	Cream cheese, plain or flavoured
Bacon, cooked and crumbled	Cucumber, use telegraph, unpeeled
Baked beans, mashed	Gherkins, chopped
Banana mashed with lemon juice	Grated cheese or soft sliced cheese
Bean salads	Green and red peppers
Beansprouts and alfalfa	Ham
Beetroot (canned)	Hard boiled egg mashed with mayonnaise
Carrot, grated	Honey
Cheese spreads	Hummus (page 30)
Cheese, processed slices	Jam
Chicken, sliced or chopped	Lemon Honey
Chocolate chips	Lettuce
Chocolate hazelnut spread	Luncheon sausage
Cold meat	Marmite etc
Coleslaw	Meat loaf, sliced
Corn chips, crushed	Nut butters
Corned beef	Olives, chopped

Pastrami, sliced or minced
Pâté (page 29)
Peanut butter
Peanuts or other chopped nuts
Pesto, basil, tomato etc
Pickled vegetables
Pineapple, crushed
Potato crisps, crushed
Potato salads
Radishes, sliced
Raw or marinated mushrooms
Roast and barbecued meat

Salami, thinly sliced
Salmon, plain and flavoured
Sardines, plain and flavoured
Sausage, sliced cooked
Smoked salmon pieces
Smoked salmon spread (page 30)
Sultanas etc, chopped
Surimi
Thinly sliced celery
Tomatoes
Tuna

Mixed Sandwich Fillings

Why settle for a single filling when so many are even better when combined! Here are some interesting ideas, using several ingredients.

Avocado (with lemon juice)/tomato
Apple/celery/chopped nuts/mayonnaise
Bacon/lettuce/avocado/tomato (BLAT)
Bacon/fried egg/lettuce/rocket
Bacon/lettuce/tomato (BLT)
Baked beans (mashed)/grated cheese
Cheese/chutney/relish/pickles
Cheese/crushed pineapple
Cheese/gherkins
Cheese/raisins
Cheese/salsa
Cheese spread/tomato/lettuce/sprouts
Cheese/dates/orange rind/juice
Cheese/marmite/lettuce or sprouts
Chicken/chopped dried apricots/cream cheese
Chicken/cranberry/lettuce
Chicken/lettuce/tomato
Chocolate spreads or chips with sultanas or raisins
Chopped or minced cooked meat/pickles or tomato sauce/shredded cabbage or lettuce
Chopped dates or other dried fruits and cream cheese
Coleslaw/raisins/cheese
Cottage cheese/tomato
Cottage cheese/banana/honey
Cream cheese/cucumber
Cream cheese/pineapple/grated carrot/raisins/ grated cheese
Cream or cottage cheese/chutney/chopped gherkin/ beansprouts
Cream cheese/chopped nuts/lettuce or alfalfa
Cream cheese/chopped sultanas/nuts
Cream cheese/lemon honey/nuts
Crunchy peanut butter/toasted chopped sunflower seeds/ chopped sultanas/honey
Egg (fried and chopped)/bacon

Egg/tomato/lettuce/sprouts
Grated carrot/raisins/lemon juice/cheese spread
Grated and/or cottage cheese/chopped celery
Grated cheese/carrot/celery/mayonnaise
Grated cheese/chopped celery/spring onion/ mayonnaise
Ham/cheese/cucumber/lettuce
Ham/coleslaw (or other salads)
Ham/cream cheese/cottage cheese/pineapple
Hawaiian: cheese/pineapple/shaved ham/lettuce
Hummus (page 30)/chopped olives
Luncheon sausage/coleslaw
Luncheon sausage/cheese/tomato sauce
Luncheon sausage (minced)/chutney/salsa
Mashed egg & mayonnaise/cress/shredded lettuce
Pastrami/cream cheese/rocket
Peanut butter/banana
Peanut butter/grated carrot/cream cheese/ chopped sultanas
Peanut butter/cream cheese/cottage cheese/ alfalfa sprouts
Peanut butter/bacon/crushed crisps
Peanut butter/tahini (in equal quantities)/mixed with honey or tofu/or chopped sunflower seeds.
Roast beef/tomato/relish/lettuce
Roast chicken/stuffing/lettuce
Salami/cream cheese/avocado
Salmon/cottage cheese/lettuce
Sardines/lemon juice/lettuce
Sausage/tomato sauce
Smoked salmon/cream cheese/horseradish
Spaghetti (in tomato sauce)/grated cheese
Sweetcorn/relish/cream cheese/lettuce
Tuna/mayonnaise/chopped cucumber /celery/ spring onion

The 'Classic' BLT

The bacon, lettuce and tomato sandwich must be one of the all time classics. It seems to us that the BLT and its cousin, the BLAT (bacon, lettuce, avocado & tomato) have just about everything you could ever want in a sandwich – colour, texture and of course fantastic flavour.

For 2 servings:
4 rashers streaky bacon
2–3 medium-sized ripe
  tomatoes
salt & pepper to taste
4 thick slices of bread
  (plain or toasted)
2–3 Tbsp mayonnaise
4 crisp cos or iceberg
  lettuce leaves
1 avocado, sliced*
  (optional)

*sprinkle the avocado with
  lemon juice to prevent
  browning

Lie the bacon rashers on 3–4 paper towels, cover with another paper towel, then microwave on High (100%) power for 3–4 minutes until the bacon is cooked. (You can fry the bacon of course, but the microwave is so easy!)

Slice the tomatoes quite thickly, then sprinkle them with salt and pepper. Spread one side of each slice of bread with mayonnaise. Cover two of the slices of bread with a generous layer of lettuce, then a layer of avocado (if using), then the sliced tomato. Lie the bacon on top, then cover with the remaining bread.

Cut the sandwiches in half if desired (secure the layers with a toothpick, if required), then serve with a napkin on the side. Enjoy!

Saté Chicken Wrap

These wraps are delicious warm, immediately after they are made, or they can be assembled and then wrapped in foil or cling film and kept cool or refrigerated until required.

For 2 servings:
250–300g boneless
  skinless chicken breast
1 clove garlic, minced
1–2 tsp grated ginger
2 tsp light soy sauce
2 tsp honey
¼–½ tsp minced red chilli
  (optional)

2 25x30cm wraps
¼ cup saté sauce
1–2 cups shredded lettuce
1 medium carrot, grated
1–2 Tbsp chopped
  coriander
2–3 Tbsp peanuts, roughly
  chopped (optional)
salt and pepper to taste

Put the chicken in a bag with the next 4 ingredients. Add chilli to taste, then massage the bag to mix everything and coat the chicken evenly. Leave to marinate for at least 10 minutes (refrigerate for longer periods).

Remove the chicken from the marinade and grill, fry or microwave (3–4 minutes on High (100%) power) until cooked through (cut in half at the thickest point to check). Leave to stand while you prepare the wraps.

Lay the wraps on a clean dry bench or board. Spread about 2 tablespoons of saté sauce over three quarters of each (leave an uncovered strip down one edge so it can be rolled up without being messy). Scatter the lettuce, then grated carrot over the sauce.

Slice the chicken and scatter this over the wraps, then sprinkle them with the coriander and some chopped peanuts if you want a bit of crunch. Season lightly with salt and pepper, then roll up (so you finish at the uncovered end). Serve with a napkin handy!

Hot off the grill

Toasted Cheese Sandwiches

Toasted cheese sandwiches are incredibly versatile. They're so quick and simple to make they can be knocked up at a few minutes' notice for a quick snack, yet are also substantial enough to form the basis of a meal – especially lunch – in their own right. What could be more inviting on a cool day?

The essential ingredients (which couldn't be much simpler) are:
- Bread (toast or sandwich sliced loaf, or sourdough loaf etc)
- A little butter or margarine, and:
- Cheese (from 'plain old' cheddar to the more exotics like camembert or brie, gruyere, raclette, telaggio, feta etc)

If you want you can add one or two extras as well (don't be too generous, or it can get messy). The classic addition is ham but there are other options like:
- Ham, prosciutto or cooked bacon
- Salami, pastrami or other cured meats
- Well drained canned tuna (sounds odd but it works!)
- Semi dried tomatoes (these seem to work better than fresh as they're not as wet so they're less prone to dribble)
- Thinly sliced avocado
- Chutney, pesto, mustard or relish

The basic method is: Spread butter or margarine thinly on two slices of bread. With buttered sides out, make a sandwich of the sliced cheese, and any optional extras, with no extra butter on the 'inside' sides.

Carefully place in a preheated frying pan on medium heat, and cook until golden brown, then turn with a fish-slice and cook the other side. Alternatively, cook them in a double-sided grill (sandwich press), preheated to medium-high. Obviously, this way they don't need to be turned. Cut into halves or quarters and eat straight away. Perfect with a bowl of soup!

Panini

In many ways, panini are just an extension of the toasted sandwich, the major difference being that because the bread is a little sturdier, it is able to cope with more generous amounts of filling. Obviously you can use panini 'buns', but exactly the same method can be applied to 'slabs' of any flattish (5cm or less thick) type loaf (foccacia, ciabatta, Turkish loaves etc.).

TO FILL: Halve the panini (or other bread) like a hamburger bun. Spread with your favourite pesto (if desired), then fill with any of the suggestions above and/or:
- Grilled vegetables (asparagus, peppers, onion, aubergine, mushrooms and/or zucchini)
- Artichoke wedges
- Cooked chicken
- Sliced cooked meats
- Smoked salmon
- Rocket
- Baby spinach leaves
- Basil leaves
- Crushed pineapple (drained)

Don't be limited by our suggestions – if you can think of other things, why not try them. Some filling combinations that go well together are:
- Sliced or shredded (cooked) chicken, camembert or brie, cranberry sauce & rocket
- Semi-dried tomatoes, feta and chopped olives or tapenade
- Cheese, char-grilled red peppers and pre-grilled portobello mushrooms
- Cheese, salami, semi-dried or fresh tomatoes, basil and/or rocket
- Creamy blue cheese, grilled asparagus & grilled mushroom
- Grilled eggplant, feta (or other cheese and grilled capsicum)
- Salami, cream cheese & avocado
- Bacon, avocado, (rocket, if desired) & tomato
- Ham, cheese and pineapple

TO COOK: Brush the outsides lightly with olive oil (if desired) then place in a preheated double-sided grill (sandwich press), on medium or high, until cheese melts and bread browns. (For best results the filled panini should be under some pressure as they cook.)

NOTE: if you have a sandwich press (contact grill etc) you can use it to pregrill the vegetables used in the above suggestion – just brush them over with plain or infused olive oil, then grill them until tender.

Quesadillas

The Mexican equivalent of a toasted sandwich or pizza! Essentially, quesadillas are flour tortillas topped or filled with a cheesy mixture, then pan fried or grilled (open or sandwiched) until crisp – all in a very short time.

Flat Quesadillas

Brush the outer edges (which will not be covered with cheese etc.) of a flour tortilla lightly with olive or canola oil. Sprinkle the remaining surface with grated cheese, and several of the following (chopped into pea-sized pieces): red onions, olives, tomatoes, red or green peppers, mushrooms, avocado, and/or cooked chicken or other meats. (Don't use too much filling – less is often better than too much!) Sprinkle these on evenly, add a little salsa if you like, then sprinkle a little more cheese on top.

Heat the tortilla flat in a heavy frypan, grill it 5–8 cm from the heat or bake it at 180°C for 5–8 minutes. However you cook it, the quesadilla is ready to be cut in wedges and eaten as soon as the tortilla has browned and crisped, the cheese has melted, and any other toppings have heated through. Cut into wedges using a heavy knife while still hot.

'Sandwiched' Quesadillas

To make thin, cheese-filled crisp tortilla "sandwiches," lightly oil two flour tortillas. With the oiled side out, put grated cheese (and any extra flavourings suggested for flat quesadillas) between them. Cut into quarters before cooking, for easier turning and handling. A sandwich press is the perfect way to cook these, but you can also pan fry or grill them, turning once to brown both sides, or bake (without turning) at 180°C for 5–8 minutes or until lightly browned and crisp.

Cut into smaller wedges soon after cooking, and eat while still warm and fairly crisp.

Eat quesadillas just as they are, or use them as dippers, especially for guacamole and salsa.

VARIATION: You may find it easier to spread filling on only half a tortilla which is to be cooked in a pan or under a grill. As soon as the tortilla has been heated enough to become flexible, flip the unfilled side over the filled side.

American Hot Dogs

OK, so these probably aren't a sandwich in a strictly true sense, but seeing as they're served in a bun we figure they're close enough! You can buy frankfurters and buns individually at many supermarkets now – so these are even easy to make at work if you have a microwave.

For each serving:
1–2 frankfurters
1–2 hot dog buns (or French bread etc)

Extras:
American-style mustard or mustard relish
tomato sauce
sautéed onions

Warm the frankfurters either by heating them in gently boiling water (don't boil them too vigorously or their skins may split), or by microwaving them on High (100%) power for about 30 seconds per sausage. (If you have a crowd to feed you can heat a considerable number of frankfurters in a slow cooker and just grab them out as required.)

Split the buns (we like to cut about three quarters of the way through the bun from the top), then pop in a frankfurter. Add your choice of 'extras' and eat.

VARIATIONS: You can buy little 'cocktail franks' – these fit really nicely in the little par-baked dinner rolls you can buy. Served like this they're fun for kids, or make up a platter of them as an easy snack to pass round while watching a game on TV.

Home-made Hamburgers

The hamburger may just be the ultimate sandwich. Not only are they quick and easy to prepare, but they taste great and are popular with children. It sounds clichéd, but hot off your own stove they really are quite different to (and much nicer than) anything you can buy!

Serve 'as is' for lunch or a light meal, or add coleslaw and potato wedges on the side for a substantial meal.

For 4 'quarter-pound' burgers:
500g minced beef
1 cup (2–3 slices bread)
    soft breadcrumbs
1 large egg
1 tsp garlic salt
black pepper to taste

To serve:
Lightly toasted buns
3–4 from list

Place all the ingredients in a large bowl, then mix thoroughly (clean hands work best for this). Divide the mixture into 4 balls then flatten these into roundish patties – it doesn't matter if they're not perfectly round.

Grill or barbecue about 20cm from the heat, turning when browned, or brown on both sides in a hot, lightly oiled frypan, then lower heat and cook until the centre is firm when pressed.

Serve in lightly toasted plain or sesame buns with three or four of the following:

> sliced tomato
> torn or shredded lettuce (or coleslaw)
> sliced cheese
> fried egg
> red, yellow and green capsicums (raw or roasted)
> sautéed mushrooms
> sliced gherkins or dill pickles
> thinly sliced red onion, crisped by soaking in cold water
> sliced avocado
> sliced beetroot
> watercress or other fresh herbs
> chilli beans and sour cream
> Of course no burger is complete without tomato sauce and/or mustard.

NOTE: You can prepare and shape the hamburger patties in advance and refrigerate them until required.

Hot Asparagus Rolls

We both absolutely love asparagus, and would eat it pretty much "breakfast, lunch and dinner" when it comes in season, if it weren't for our respective spouses who both enjoy it but not to the same degree! These simple but delicious rolls are one way we've been enjoying it lately.

For 2 servings:
200–250g asparagus
2 tsp butter
½ lemon, zest and juice
2–3 Tbsp mayonnaise
½ French stick or two long
    rolls
salt and pepper to taste

Trim or break any tough ends from the asparagus. Place it in an oven bag then roll the bag up loosely, then microwave for 1½–2 minutes on High (100%) power (or boil gently) until tender. Drain (if required) then add the butter and the juice of half a lemon.

Put the mayonnaise in a small bowl and stir in the lemon zest. Cut the bread into two pieces (warm it in the microwave first if you want), each about as long as the asparagus and spit it along the middle. Spread half the mayonnaise on each roll, then lay the asparagus spears on top. Season to taste with salt and pepper, then enjoy!

VARIATION: Try adding 40–50g shaved ham along with the asparagus.

Steak Burritos

Try these Tex-Mex steak 'sandwiches' and you'll be hooked – they're delicious and good fun to make and eat too! (The steak is great cooked on a summer barbecue.)

For 3–4 servings:
400–500g rump or Scotch fillet steak
2 cloves garlic, minced
2 Tbsp lime juice
1 Tbsp each soy sauce and olive oil
1 tsp each cumin and oreganum
½ tsp minced chilli

Salsa
1 medium avocado, diced
2 medium tomatoes, diced
1 Tbsp lemon or lime juice
1 clove garlic, minced
1–2 Tbsp chopped coriander
salt and pepper to taste

To serve:
6–8 large flour tortillas, warmed
½ small red onion, finely sliced
½ medium lettuce, finely shredded
1 medium carrot grated
1 cup grated cheese
hot chilli sauce, optional

Place the steak in a sturdy plastic bag with the next seven ingredients. Massage the bag so the steak is coated with the mixture on all sides, then squeeze out as much air as possible and leave to marinate for at least 20 minutes (overnight is OK if you like to work ahead).

About 20–30 minutes before you want to eat, prepare the salsa by combining all the ingredients in a medium sized bowl and stirring gently to combine. Leave the salsa to stand while you preheat over a high heat a heavy frypan, griddle pan or barbecue and organize the accompaniments.

Non-stick spray the pan/griddle/barbecue, then cook the steak for 2–3 minutes per side. Remove it from the heat and leave to stand for 5 minutes before slicing thinly with a knife held at about 45° to the board.

To serve, lie a tortilla on a plate or board, arrange some onion, lettuce, carrot and cheese in a line across the middle, then top with a generous mound of the sliced steak and a dollop of the salsa. Add a dash of chilli sauce if you like, then fold the bottom end up and the sides in to form a manageable parcel. Hold with both hands while you eat!

Falafel in Pita Pockets

Falafel are crunchy little chickpea patties, and are delicious served stuffed into a pita bread pocket with some salad and a little tahini-yoghurt sauce.

For 3–4 servings:
1 cup chickpeas
½ medium onion
2 cloves garlic, peeled
½ cup chopped parsley
2 tsp cumin
½ tsp allspice
1 tsp salt
olive or canola oil to fry

To serve:
3–4 20cm pita breads
lettuce leaves
quartered cherry tomatoes
thinly sliced red onion

Place the chickpeas in a bowl and cover them with about 4 cups boiling water and leave to soak for 8 hours (or overnight), then drain well.

Put the onion and garlic in a food processor and process until finely chopped. Add the chickpeas and process until coarsely chopped then add the remaining ingredients, except the oil. Process again until the mixture is about the texture of dryish crunchy peanut butter.

Divide the mixture into quarters, then divide each quarter into four smaller 'blobs'. Working with (clean) wet hands to prevent sticking, shape each blob into a flat round patty about 1cm thick and 4–5cm across.

Heat 2–3mm of oil over a medium heat in a non-stick frypan, then gently add four to six of the patties and cook for 3–4 minutes per side until crisp and brown (reduce the heat if they are browning too fast – they do need to be cooked through). Drain the cooked falafel on paper towels.

To serve: Warm the pita breads, then cut them in half crossways and open them to form pockets. Stuff a few lettuce leaves, some tomato pieces, a little onion and two of the falafel into each pocket. Add a spoonful or two of tahini sauce (below) to each and serve with napkins handy.

NOTE: The falafel can be cooked ahead and reheated gently in a frypan or the microwave before serving.

Tahini-Yoghurt Sauce
½ cup natural unsweetened yoghurt
2 Tbsp tahini
2 Tbsp lemon or lime juice
½ teaspoon paprika
salt and pepper to taste

Measure the first four ingredients into a small bowl and whisk until smooth, then season to taste with salt. Serve spooned into the falafel pita pockets.

Spread it on
(Dips & Spreads)

Some of these can stand alone to form the basis of a light meal or at least a hearty snack (hummus, chicken liver pâté, smoked salmon spread), while some of the others (like pesto and mayonnaise) are really just those little things that make life more interesting. All can be used very simply to transform sandwiches, rolls etc from the mundane to something quite special.

Herbed Chicken-liver Pâté

This easily made, smooth and creamy mixture is the most popular pâté we have ever made. It freezes well too. A container of this pâté, some bread or crackers and a bottle of wine makes a super easy picnic, or use it as a delicious sandwich spread.

For about 375g, or 2 cups:

100g butter
1–2 cloves garlic, minced
350–400g chicken livers
2 fresh or dried bay leaves if available
2–4 Tbsp finely chopped fresh herbs such as thyme and oreganum
2 Tbsp chopped fresh parsley
2 Tbsp Thai sweet chilli sauce
¼ cup cream
2–4 Tbsp brandy or sherry (or a mixture of both)
freshly ground pepper
½ tsp salt

Melt the butter over moderate heat in a fairly large non-stick frypan. Stir in the garlic then add the chicken livers, straight from their pack. (Use a little more or less if desired.)

Add the bay leaves, herbs and chilli sauce and cook over low to moderate heat until the chicken livers are cooked right through, about 5 minutes. As they cook, chop them into small pieces (in the pan) with kitchen scissors – when the cut surfaces show no pink, they are ready.

Add the cream and bring mixture back to the boil, then add the sherry and/or brandy and simmer for a minute longer. Turn off the heat, and add the pepper and salt.

Remove the bay leaves, then purée the hot mixture in a food processor. Sieve the puréed mixture, a third at a time, to remove herbs and any fibrous pieces. (Bang the sieve above the bowl for easiest sieving.) Pour into suitable containers, then cover and chill until firm.

Pour extra melted butter (with peppercorns or small bay leaves if desired) over the cold pâté if desired. Refrigerate up to a week or freeze for up to 2 months.

Hummus, Plain or 'Fancy'

Good old hummus is a delicious and versatile mixture. Served with vegetable crudités and wedges of pita bread it makes a delicious snack or light meal at home, school or work, but it is also delicious used as a spread in sandwiches and rolls. (Wheatmeal bread, hummus and sliced olives make a delicious sandwich!)

'Plain' hummus is just fine, but when you feel like something a little different, try the Pumpkin & Peanut version given below too.

For about 1½ cups:
1 large clove garlic
300g can chickpeas,
   rinsed and drained
2 Tbsp tahini
2 Tbsp lemon juice
2–3 Tbsp olive oil
¼–½ teaspoon salt
water to thin (if required)

Place the garlic and chickpeas in a blender or food processor, fitted with a metal chopping blade, and process until finely chopped. Add the tahini and lemon juice. Process until evenly mixed, then add two tablespoons of the oil and ¼ teaspoon of salt. Process until very smooth stopping once or twice to scrape down the sides and adding the extra oil and/or water to thin to the desired consistency, if required. Taste and add a little extra salt if needed.

Serve immediately with warmed pita wedges, crackers and/or vegetable (carrot, cucumber, celery and cauliflower) crudités, or transfer to an airtight container and store in the fridge for up to a week.

Pumpkin & Peanut Hummus (pictured opposite).
Place 100g peeled and cubed pumpkin in a small microwave bowl, cover and microwave on high (100%) for two minutes. Add the cooked pumpkin to the processor with the chickpeas and garlic. Replace the tahini with 2 tablespoons peanut butter and for a slight twist, add ¼ teaspoon curry powder as well, then proceed as above.

Hot-smoked Salmon Dip or Spread

This delicious quickly made dip has the attractive colour and appealing flavour of hot-smoked salmon. It may be used as a popular spread, for special occasion sandwiches etc. too.

For about 1½ cups:
100–150g hot or cold
   smoked salmon
250g carton cream cheese
2 Tbsp lemon juice
1–2 Tbsp capers
1–2 Tbsp horseradish
   cream (optional)
about 2 Tbsp chopped
   parsley, dill or chives
   (optional)
salt and pepper to taste

Put the salmon, cream cheese and lemon juice into a food processor and process until well mixed but not completely smooth. Add the capers, horseradish (if using) and the chopped herbs of your choice, and process again, just enough to mix.

Season to taste then cover and refrigerate until required. (Although it tastes good when eaten straight away, its flavour is even better after a couple of hours.)

Serve spread on crusty bread, crackers, etc., as a dip for vegetable crudités, or with lettuce or cucumber as an easy sandwich/roll filling.

Mexican Cheese & Tomato Dip

This mixture makes a spicy and delicious hot or warm dip to serve with corn chips and vegetable crudités, perfect for a snack or light meal, or, when cold makes an interesting spread for sandwiches, rolls, crackers etc.

For 4–8 servings:
1 medium-sized onion
1 green pepper
1 Tbsp canola or other oil
1 tsp ground cumin
½ tsp ground coriander
  seeds
¼–½ tsp chilli powder
  (optional)
425g can whole or diced
  tomatoes
1 Tbsp flour
2 cups grated tasty cheese
¼ –½ cup low-fat sour
  cream
coriander leaves or spring
  onions for garnish

Halve then peel the onion. Halve the pepper, and remove and discard all seeds and pith. Chop both into small (about 5mm) cubes. Cook these in the oil, without browning, for 3–4 minutes. Stir in the cumin, ground coriander and chilli powder (if using) and cook a minute longer.

Bring to the boil and add the contents of the can of tomatoes. (If you use a can of whole rather than chopped tomatoes, break them up.)

Toss the flour through the cheese, then stir into the hot tomato mixture until melted and smooth. Do not bring the mixture to the boil after the cheese has been added.

Serve hot, in a shallow dipping bowl, garnished with chopped coriander leaves or finely chopped spring onions. Serve surrounded by corn chips and vegetable crudités for dipping.

Alternatively, allow to cool, then transfer to an airtight container and store in the fridge for up to a week to use as a roll or sandwich filling.

VARIATION: Make without the green pepper if necessary. It is still very good! Replace ground coriander seeds with the same amount of dried oregano if you like.

Mayonnaise

We think that good mayonnaise must be one of the ultimate sandwich spreads. It is much easier to 'apply' than butter or margarine and goes so well with almost any savoury filling.

While you can now buy good quality mayonnaise, it's comparatively expensive for something so quick and easy to make in the food processor. This sauce is delicious and versatile. It puts most bought mayonnaise to shame!

For about 1½ cups:
1 egg
½ tsp each salt and sugar
1 tsp Dijon or mild mustard
2 Tbsp wine vinegar
about 1 cup olive or
  canola oil

Measure the first five ingredients into a food processor or blender. Turn on and add the oil in a thin stream until the mayonnaise is as thick and creamy as you like it.

Keep in a covered container in the refrigerator for up to 10 days.

Basil Pesto

Traditional basil pesto is almost impossible to beat. It is one of those little extras that is incredibly versatile – plain or mixed with mayonnaise, sour cream or cream cheese it really gives sandwiches and rolls a lift. For a really quick and easy meal, simply stir it through cooked pasta. (One batch makes about enough for 8 servings).

For 1–1½ cups:
4 cloves garlic, peeled
4 cups (about 150g)
   fresh basil, large stems
   removed
½ cup pine nuts
½ cup grated Parmesan
   cheese
about ½ cup olive oil
salt to taste

Put the peeled garlic, basil leaves and pine nuts in a food processor and process until well chopped. Add the grated Parmesan and half a cup of olive oil and process again until well mixed. Start adding the extra olive oil a tablespoon at a time until you have a fairly smooth paste that just holds its shape.

Salt to taste, then transfer into airtight containers for storage. Pour a little extra oil on top of each container to help prevent browning. We like to leave pesto to stand for at least an hour before serving, so the flavours can blend.

To use as a pasta sauce alone, simply toss pesto through freshly cooked pasta (allow about ¼ of a cup of pesto per 100g serving of uncooked pasta). Served over fresh pasta with a good salad and a bottle of your favourite wine, this makes a really simple and elegant meal.

Sun-dried Tomato Pesto

Sun-dried tomatoes are a real treat, and having them on hand in the form of this rich and flavourful spread is a real bonus. Make the full mixture and keep it in the fridge until required. Like basil pesto it's incredibly versatile – spread it 'as is' or mixed with cream cheese or mayo onto rolls and sandwiches. Try it spread on bruschetta or crostini, as a pasta sauce (thinned with a little cream or oil) or even as the tomato base for pizza.

For about 1¼ cups:
¼ cup pine nuts
1 cup drained sun-dried
   tomatoes
1 clove garlic, peeled
about ¼ cup olive oil, or
   oil from the sun-dried
   tomatoes
1 Tbsp balsamic vinegar
salt to taste

Toast the pine nuts until they are golden brown in a dry frying pan or under the grill. Leave to cool for a few minutes then put these in a food processor with the tomatoes and garlic. Process until everything is coarsely chopped, then add the oil and vinegar. Blend until the mixture reaches the consistency you like the most, from slightly chunky to a smooth paste, adding the extra oil if you think it looks too dry.

Transfer the mixture into a clean airtight container and store in the refrigerator for 1–2 weeks.

To serve four as a pasta sauce, mix ½ cup pesto with ¼ cup cream or oil, then stir through 400g of cooked pasta. Sprinkle with some shaved or grated parmesan and serve!

Salad Days

(Cool Salads for warmer weather)

A salad can easily form the basis of a meal whether you are at home, at work, or just out and about! These salads are all fairly substantial, and for the most part they are sturdy enough to withstand being made ahead and packed for travel (although they should be packed in insulated containers, or stored in a fridge until required).

Couscous & Salmon Salad

This is a very handy salad – not only is it very tasty, but it can be made ahead (although the lettuce does get a little tired if made too far in advance), or as long as you have access to boiling water and a knife it can be made 'on the spot'.

For 2–3 large servings:
220g can salmon
1 cup salmon liquid plus
  water
½ cup (instant) couscous
½ tsp salt
2 Tbsp lemon juice
1–2 Tbsp olive oil
½ cup diced, deseeded
  cucumber
2 tomatoes, diced
1–2 cups finely sliced
  lettuce
freshly ground black
  pepper

Open and drain the salmon collecting the liquid. Add enough water to make it up to 1 cup.

Measure the couscous into a large bowl. Tip the liquid into a small pot (or microwave bowl), heat to boiling then pour it over the couscous and set aside to cool for five minutes (or so).

Tip the salmon into a small bowl and add the lemon juice and olive oil. Leave the salmon to stand for a minute then stir in the diced vegetables.

When the couscous has cooled 'fluff' it up with a fork, then add the salmon–vegetable mixture. Don't add the lettuce until you are ready to serve, or it will go soft. Mix everything and add a good grind of black pepper. Serve immediately.

Ham & Pasta Salad with Lemon-Mustard Dressing

Ham and pasta salads are hardly a new idea – but they are always popular! This delicious salad will stand alone as a complete meal, but also makes a great addition to a summer buffet.

For 4 large servings:
250g pasta (spirals, bows
  etc)
150–200g sliced ham, cut
  into narrow strips
2–3 sticks celery, sliced
2 medium tomatoes, sliced
½ small red onion, diced
1–2 Tbsp chopped fresh
  chives or parsley to
  garnish

Dressing:
½ cup mayonnaise
finely grated rind of 1
  lemon
¼ cup lemon juice
2 Tbsp olive or canola oil
1 Tbsp wholegrain mustard
½ tsp salt
black pepper to taste

Cook the pasta in plenty of lightly salted boiling water. As soon as it is cooked, drain then cool the pasta by rinsing it in plenty of cold water. (Overcooking the pasta will result in a soggy, unpleasant salad.)

Prepare the dressing by whisking the first six dressing ingredients together in a large bowl, then adding black pepper to taste.

Add the cooled drained pasta, ham and prepared vegetables to the dressing and stir gently to combine. Garnish with the chopped herbs and serve immediately, or store in the fridge until required (salad can be prepared several hours in advance if desired). Pack in an insulated container if taking for lunch.

Orzo & Feta Salad

Orzo (sometimes also called risoni) is little rice-shaped pasta. Because it is shaped into little grains it is relatively solid so it is well suited to withstanding the rigours of being packed, and travelling!

For 3–4 large servings:
250g orzo or risoni
2 medium tomatoes
½ red pepper
½ green pepper
100g feta
2 spring onions
about 12 pitted kalamata
    olives

Dressing:
3 Tbsp olive oil
1 lemon, zest and juice
1 Tbsp wholegrain mustard
1 clove garlic, minced
½ tsp salt
pepper to taste

Put the orzo on to cook in a large pot of rapidly boiling, lightly salted water. While the orzo cooks, prepare the remaining ingredients.

Cut the tomatoes and deseeded peppers into 7–10mm cubes. Crumble the feta into roughly similar sized pieces, and thinly slice the green parts of the spring onions (don't add the white parts unless you want a strong onion flavour), and roughly chop the pitted olives.

To make the dressing, measure the olive oil into a small bowl, finely grate the yellow zest from the lemon and add it to the oil, then squeeze and add the juice. Add the remaining ingredients, then whisk until thoroughly combined.

When the orzo is cooked (12–15 minutes), drain it, then rinse with cold water until it is cool and drain again. Tip the drained orzo back into the pot, add the vegetables, feta and dressing and stir gently until evenly mixed.

Transfer to serving bowl/s and serve immediately, or refrigerate until required (it will keep for up to 2 days). Transport in an air-tight, insulated container.

American-style Potato Salad

This ever-popular, mildly flavoured salad travels well (although it should be kept cool) and makes a great lunch! It is very good 'plain', but can also be 'dressed-up' by the addition of some optional extras.

For 3–4 servings:
1kg waxy or new potatoes
2 Tbsp white wine vinegar
2 Tbsp olive or canola oil
½ cup mayonnaise
about 2 tbsp milk or lemon
    juice
2 tsp white wine vinegar
2 sticks celery, sliced
¼ cup chopped parsley
2 spring onions, sliced
salt and pepper to taste

Optional Extras:
chopped hard-boiled egg
sliced frankfurter or bier
    stick
sliced or chopped gherkins
crispy fried bacon
roasted pumpkin seeds

Scrub the potatoes, then boil them gently until just cooked. Drain the potatoes, then return them to the cooking pot and add the first measure of vinegar and the oil. Toss gently to coat with the vinegar and oil, then leave to stand until room temperature.

Thin the mayonnaise with the milk or lemon juice and the vinegar. Slice or cube the cooled potatoes into a large bowl, then add the celery, sliced spring onions, chopped parsley and the mayonnaise mixture (and one or two of the optional extras, if desired). Mix gently, without breaking up the potato too much.

We like to serve this at about room temperature, but if you're making it in advance, it should be refrigerated until shortly before it is required. Serve as is or garnished with some more parsley and/or chives.

Transport in an air-tight, insulated container.

Peanutty Noodle Salad

This salad makes a delicious meal on its own, but if you want something more substantial, add a little cooked or smoked chicken.

For 4–6 servings:
250g fine or ribbon egg
  noodles
1 large carrot
½ small cucumber
1–2 spring onions
1 cup bean sprouts
1–2 cups sliced cabbage

Dressing:
3 Tbsp peanut butter
2 Tbsp light soy
2 Tbsp lime or lemon juice
1 Tbsp each sesame oil,
  canola oil and honey
1 clove garlic, minced
1–2 tsp grated fresh ginger
½–1 tsp minced red chilli
2–3 Tbsp chopped
  coriander (optional)
salt to taste

Put the noodles on to cook in plenty of lightly salted boiling water. While the noodles cook, prepare the remaining ingredients.

Make the dressing by measuring all the ingredients except the salt into a screw-top jar and shaking until well combined. Season to taste with salt.

Grate the carrot and halve the cucumber lengthways, scoop out and discard the seeds, then julienne. Thinly slice the spring onion/s.

As soon as the noodles are just cooked (over-cooked noodles will be soggy and weak), drain, then rinse them well with cold water. Return the noodles to the cooking pot or a large bowl and toss with a little oil, then add the vegetables and dressing and stir gently until combined. If possible leave to stand for 15–30 minutes before serving, garnished with a little extra chopped coriander.

Use immediately, refrigerate until required and/or pack in a tightly sealed insulated container.

Oriental Noodle Salad

This simple salad may sound a little unusual, but once you've tried it you'll agree it really is good!

For 2–3 servings:
2 cups water
1 packet 2-Minute Noodles
1 Tbsp wine vinegar
2 Tbsp oil
1 cup finely shredded
  cabbage
1 carrot cut in thin strips
2 celery stalks, sliced thinly
1–2 spring onions, sliced

Boil water in a pot. Add broken noodles. Boil for 2 minutes then drain.

While the noodles cook, prepare the vegetables. Mix the flavour sachet contents together with the vinegar and oil.

When the noodles are cooked, drain them then return to the cooking pot or a bowl. Stir in the prepared vegetables and the oil and vinegar mixture. Serve immediately, or pack into an airtight container and refrigerate or icy cool in an insulated container until required.

VARIATION/S: Nice additions include: ¼–½ cup chopped peanuts, or ½–1 cup of cooked chicken or ham. For a more pronounced Asian flavour add a sprinkling of sesame oil and soy sauce.

Nutty Brown Rice Salad

The brown rice, sesame oil and peanuts give this 'travel friendly' salad a delicious nutty flavour. It's lovely just made and still warm, but is equally good made ahead and served cool from the fridge. If you're making it to take to work you may want to omit the garlic in the dressing.

For 2–3 large servings:
1 cup brown rice
1¾ cups boiling water
½ tsp salt
1 medium carrot
½ red pepper
2 spring onions
½ cup frozen peas
½–¾ cup roasted peanuts
1–2 Tbsp chopped
   coriander

Dressing:
1 Tbsp sesame oil
1 Tbsp canola oil
1 Tbsp Kikkoman soy
   sauce
1 Tbsp white wine vinegar
1 clove garlic, minced
1–2 tsp grated ginger
1 tsp brown sugar
¼ tsp minced red chilli

Place the rice, boiling water and salt in a large microwave bowl, then cover and microwave on Medium-High (70%) power for 25–30 minutes, or until the water is absorbed and the rice tender.

While the rice cooks, grate or finely dice the carrot and dice the red pepper. Thinly slice the green parts of the spring onions (if you want a stronger onion flavour, slice the white parts too).

Make the dressing measuring all the ingredients in a small bowl (or screw topped jar) and whisking (or shaking) until combined.

As soon as the rice is cooked, stir in the frozen peas (this 'cooks' the peas, and cools the rice). Add the peanuts, prepared vegetables, chopped coriander and the dressing, then stir gently to combine.

Serve immediately, or allow to cool then refrigerate until required (will keep for up to 2 days). Pack in an insulated container for transport.

Curried Chicken & Kumara Salad

This substantial and delicious salad does involve three different stages, but all of them are easy, and the result is worth the effort.

For 2–3 large servings:

2 Tbsp plain unsweetened yoghurt
1 Tbsp sweet mango chutney
1 tsp curry powder
2 cloves garlic, minced
300–400g boneless, skinless chicken
500g kumara
2–3 sticks celery, sliced
½ cup roasted cashews or peanuts, roughly chopped
¼–½ cup chopped dates
¼ cup chopped coriander

Dressing:

½ cup plain unsweetened yoghurt
1–2 Tbsp sweet mango chutney
1 tsp curry powder
1 tsp salt

Put the first measure of yoghurt, chutney and curry powder and the chopped garlic into a plastic bag. Add the chicken, then massage the bag so the chicken is evenly coated with the marinade. Set aside for at least 15 minutes (refrigerate for longer periods).

Peel the kumara and cut into 2–3cm cubes. Cook until tender either by microwaving on High (100%) in a covered container for 7–10 minutes, or by boiling gently, then drain (if required) and leave to cool to room temperature.

Cook the chicken by grilling 5–10 cm from the heat, for 5–10 minutes on each side (depending on thickness) or until the outside has browned and the juices run clear when the chicken is pierced at the thickest part. Leave chicken to stand for 5–10 minutes, then cut into bite-sized pieces.

While the chicken cooks, stir the dressing ingredients together and prepare the remaining salad ingredients.

Place the cooled kumara, chicken and remaining ingredients (reserving a little of the coriander to garnish) in a large bowl, drizzle with dressing, then toss gently to combine.

Garnish with the reserved coriander and serve immediately or refrigerate until required. Transport in an insulated container.

Portable Packages

(Pies, Pizza, Calzone & Sushi)

Whichever of this somewhat eclectic collection of pies and packages you choose to make, we're sure you'll have some delighted recipients. From tasty morsels wrapped in tender golden pastry, to delicacies wrapped in glossy dark nori, these parcels lend themselves to being transported to be enjoyed, whether it's in the backyard, on a windswept beach or hilltop, or at work!

Patricia's Pork Pie

So quick and easy to make, and absolutely delicious served hot, warm, or cold – perfect for a picnic or packed lunch.

For 4–6 servings:

400g savoury short pastry or 1 recipe "Easy Flakey Pastry", page 42
3 thick slices wholegrain bread
2 eggs, lightly beaten
1 large onion, peeled and roughly chopped
about 6 leaves fresh sage or ½ tsp dried sage, crumbled
about ¼ cup chopped parsley
1 tsp salt
2 Tbsp sherry, optional
400–500g minced pork

Preheat the oven to 200°C.

Cut the block of (thawed) pastry in half crosswise. Working on a lightly floured surface, roll each half out on a floured board, using a floured rolling pin, to form two 30–35cm squares. Leave to stand while you make the filling.

Break the bread into chunky pieces, crumb these in a food processor, then remove.

Add the eggs (reserve about 1 tablespoonful to use as glaze), the roughly chopped onion, sage leaves, parsley, salt and sherry to the food processor, then process until the onion is finely chopped. Add the crumbs and minced pork, broken up into 4 or 5 chunks, then process in short bursts until everything is evenly mixed.

Put one square of pastry on a baking paper or teflon lined baking sheet, and spread the filling on the centre of it, in a 25cm square. Moisten the uncovered pastry around the filling with cold water, and place the other sheet on top, pressing it down around the meat. Cut a dozen or so air vents over the filling. Trim pastry edges evenly, fold about 1cm back under, then crimp or flute the edge.

Brush the pastry with the reserved egg mixed with a teaspoon of water. If you like, cut trimmings into shapes, arrange on top and brush with egg. Bake at 200°C for 15 minutes, then at 180°C for a further 30 minutes.

Picnic Pie

This pie is much greater than 'the sum of the parts' – while it may not sound too interesting on paper it really is delicious, and can be eaten warm or cold. It is perfect for picnics or packed lunches.

For 4–6 servings:

2 sheets (300g total) pre-rolled flakey pastry
500g sausage meat
400g can whole tomatoes, in juice
½ cup frozen peas (optional)
3 large eggs
½ tsp salt
black pepper to taste
1 cup grated cheese

Preheat the oven to 180°C

Roll one sheet of the pastry out to about 35cm square, then ease it into a non-stick sprayed 21cm square cake tin, so it covers the bottom and sides.

Break the sausage meat into 9–12 pieces, and arrange these in the pie shell (it doesn't matter if there are gaps in between the blobs). Open and drain the tomatoes, then cut each tomato into quarters and scatter these (and the peas, if using) over and between the sausage meat. Lightly beat the eggs together adding the salt and a grind of pepper. Pour the egg mixture into the pie, reserving 1–2 tablespoons to use as a glaze. Scatter the grated cheese over the fillings.

Moisten the exposed edge of the pastry with a little milk or water, then cover with the remaining pastry sheet. Trim the edges about 1cm beyond the edge of the tin. Fold this back under the lower crust and decorate the edge with a fork or fingers. Cut several slits near the centre to let steam escape, then brush the surface with the reserved egg.

Bake for 40 minutes, reducing the heat if the top is getting too brown.

Easy 'Flakey' Pastry

This isn't a true puff pastry, but it is richer and flakier than a 'standard' savoury short pastry – and if you have a food processor it's very easy to make.

For about 400g pastry:
enough for 1 galette,
(below, or 2x23cm quiches
or flans):
1½ cups flour
½ tsp baking powder
100g cold butter
½ cup cold milk
1 tsp white wine vinegar

Measure the flour and baking powder into a food processor fitted with a metal chopping blade. Cut the cold butter into 9 cubes and add to the flour. Process in short bursts until the butter is cut into pieces about 5mm across.

Mix the milk and vinegar, then processing in brief pulses slowly pour in just enough liquid to make the pastry mixture look like breadcrumbs that will just form a ball when gently squeezed (stop frequently to test this). Press the dough into a disk and chill for about 10 minutes.

Goat Cheese & Olive Galette

A galette is somewhere between a pie and a pizza – there's no pie plate and the pastry is folded back over the filling, so it is part open and part closed.

For 3–4 servings:
1 recipe "Easy Flakey
    Pastry"
2 Tbsp olive or canola oil
2 medium onions, peeled,
    halved and sliced
1 medium red capsicum
    (pepper), cored and
    sliced
2 medium tomatoes,
    cubed
1 tsp dried thyme
salt and pepper to taste
about 12 Kalamata olives
50–100g goat cheese (feta
    or chèvre)

Make the pastry (according to the instructions above) and leave to chill while you prepare the filling mixture. Preheat the oven to180°C.

Heat the oil in a large frypan. Add the onion and cook over a medium–high heat, stirring occasionally, for 3–4 minutes until the onion begins to brown. Stir in the capsicum, tomatoes and thyme and cook for 5–6 minutes longer, stirring frequently. Remove from the heat and season to taste with salt and pepper.

Working on a lightly floured surface, roll the pastry out to form a round about 45–50cm across. Roll the pastry around your rolling pin and lift it onto a teflon or baking paper lined oven tray. Spread the filling mix over the middle 30cm or so, then sprinkle the filling with the olives and crumbled cheese. Fold the uncovered pastry edges back over the filling, making five or six tucks around the inner edge so it will sit flat.

Place in the middle of the oven and bake for 15–20 minutes until the pastry is golden brown. Remove from the oven and allow to cool for several minutes before serving with a simple salad alongside.

Vegetable Flan (or Quiche)

You can use the same basic recipe to make a flan or quiche from a wide variety of different cooked vegetables, depending what you have on hand! This recipe will make a deep 17cm flan or a shallower (and therefore quicker cooking) 23cm one.

For a 17–23cm flan or quiche:

1 uncooked pastry crust (use bought savoury short pastry, or homemade pastry)
3 eggs
½ cup sour cream
¼ cup milk
½ tsp salt
pepper to taste
1½ cups grated cheese
1–1½ cups well drained cooked vegetables (asparagus, broccoli, corn, mushrooms, spinach etc.)
paprika to dust (optional)

Preheat the oven to 200°C.

Thinly roll out the bought or homemade pastry to line your pie plate.

Whisk the eggs, sour cream, milk, salt, pepper and 1 cup of the grated cheese together in a medium sized bowl.

Arrange the well drained vegetable (or vegetable mixture) of your choice in the pie shell, then carefully pour in the egg mixture. Sprinkle the top with the remaining grated cheese and dust with paprika (if desired).

Bake in the middle of the oven for 20 minutes at 200°C, then reduce the heat to 180°C and bake until the filling is set in the middle, usually around 10 minutes.

VARIATIONS: You can replace up to ½ cup of the vegetables with an equal amount of chopped ham or smoked chicken, or well drained canned tuna or salmon.

Self-crusting Potato & Vegetable Quiche

Potatoes give this 'quiche' bulk, while your selected vegetable/s add colour and flavour. If you are planning to make this to cut into pieces for packed lunches, consider using a square tin – it makes wrapping it easier.

For 4–6 servings:

1 Tbsp oil or butter
1 medium–large onion, peeled and diced
2 cloves of garlic, peeled and chopped
3 eggs
1 cup milk
¾ tsp salt
½ cup self raising flour
2 cooked potatoes, cut in 1cm cubes
1 cup well drained cooked vegetables (asparagus, broccoli, char-grilled peppers, corn, chopped semi-dried tomatoes, spinach and/or mushrooms, or a mixture)
1 cup grated cheese
sliced tomato to garnish (optional)

Preheat the oven to 220°C (or 210°C for fan-bake).

Heat the butter or oil in a non-stick pan. Add the onion and garlic and cook, stirring frequently until the onion is soft, then remove from the heat and leave to cool.

Add the eggs, milk and salt to the cooled onion mixture and stir until well mixed. Measure the self raising flour into a large bowl. Pour the egg and onion mixture into the flour and stir with a fork until just combined (the idea is that some of the flour settles to the bottom during cooking to form a crust, but if overmixed, this doesn't happen). Add the cubed potatoes, well drained vegetables and grated cheese.

Non-stick spray a 20–23cm metal (this helps crust formation) tin. Pour the quiche mixture into the tin, then decorate the top with thinly sliced tomato (if desired). Bake at 220°C (or 210°C for fan-bake) for 20–30 minutes or until golden brown and set in the centre.

Allow to stand for 5 minutes before turning out of the pan and cutting.

Easy Vegetable & Feta Tart

In terms of ease and preparation, this is really very similar to a pizza. Delicious and attractive, it makes a great dish to serve to company or for elegant picnics.

For 4–6 servings:

2 sheets (about 300g total) pre-rolled flakey pastry
2 Tbsp tomato paste
1 Tbsp pesto, optional
1 Tbsp water
½ tsp marjoram
½ tsp salt
black pepper to taste
250g small ripe tomatoes
1 small or ½ medium red onion
½ medium yellow or red pepper, julienned
1 medium zucchini, julienned
1–2 cloves minced garlic (optional)
about 8 basil leaves, roughly shredded
2 Tbsp olive oil
100g feta cheese, crumbled
salt and pepper to taste

Preheat the oven to 200°C.

Lie each pastry sheet on a baking tray, then without cutting right through, run a knife around the sheet about 1cm inside the edge of each, marking out a smaller square.

Mix together the tomato paste, pesto, water, marjoram, salt and black pepper. Spread this mixture evenly over the pastry squares, trying to keep the outer borders clear.

Cut each of the tomatoes and the onion into 6–8 small wedges. Combine the vegetables, garlic (if using) and shredded basil in a bowl. Add the olive oil and toss gently until evenly coated with oil. Spread the prepared vegetables over the paste-covered bases, then sprinkle evenly with the crumbled feta. Season with salt and pepper to taste, then bake at 200°C for 10 minutes, then reduce the heat to 180°C for another 10–15 minutes or until the crust is golden brown.

Serve hot, warm or cold with a green salad or as part of a picnic buffet.

Sausage Rolls

They're not exactly glamorous, but bring them out and you'll find that sausage rolls are remarkably popular. You can buy perfectly good ones frozen, but it's just not the same as making your own!

For 8 large or 20–24 small sausage rolls:

1 small onion
2 slices bread
1 clove garlic
1 Tbsp tomato paste
500g sausage meat
½ tsp salt
2 sheets (about 300g total) pre-rolled puff pastry
1 egg, lightly beaten

Preheat the oven to 200°C.

Chop the onion finely, then place it in a small bowl and microwave on High (100%) power for 1 minute (this makes the flavour a bit milder). Tear the bread into chunks and place in a food processor and process until finely crumbed, then add the peeled garlic, the tomato paste and the onion. Process again until well mixed.

Add the sausage meat (breaking it into 6–8 pieces will mean it mixes more easily) and salt. Process in short bursts until evenly mixed.

Take one of the pastry sheets and place it on a lightly floured surface. Cut the sheet in half (this should give two rectangles measuring about 22x11cm) and roll each out so it is a little thinner and measures about 26x15cm. Repeat with the other pastry sheet, so you have four long rectangles.

Working with wet hands (to stop sticking), divide the filling into quarters. Take the first quarter and gently squeeze it into a sausage 2–3cm thick and long enough to reach longways down one of the pastry sheets. Lie the 'sausage' down the middle of one of the pastry sheets, fold one edge of the pastry over the filling, then lightly brush the exposed pastry edge with water and fold up and over the filling so it overlaps the other pastry edge (don't wrap too tightly – the filling will expand a little as it cooks, and the pastry will shrink). Turn the roll over and rest it on the seam while you prepare the remaining rolls.

With a sharp knife, cut each of the long rolls in half for large rolls or into 5–6 pieces for bite sized rolls and arrange these on a baking paper covered baking sheet. Brush each little roll with a little of the lightly beaten egg, then place in the oven and bake for 25–30 minutes or until golden brown and the filling is cooked. (Reduce the heat a little after about 15 minutes if you think they're browning too fast.) Remove from the oven and allow to cool a little before serving.

Pieburgers

This American recipe is easier to make than regular meat pies, and is popular with all age groups. As the filling is not precooked they're really simple to make, and so versatile. Once cooked the pieburgers can be eaten immediately, or cooled and packed for a picnic; alternatively, freeze them to take for lunches (enjoy them cold or reheat in a microwave).

For 9 'Pieburgers':

2 sheets (about 300g total) pre-rolled flakey pastry
500g minced beef
1 pkt (about 25g) Mushroom Sauce
or 1 pkt (about 30g) French Onion Soup
¼ cup tomato sauce
2 Tbsp flour
1 egg, lightly beaten
½ cup grated cheese

Preheat the oven to 200°C.

Lightly roll the chilled pastry out into two squares, one about 30cm square, and the other slightly (3–5cm) larger.

Put the mince, soup mix, tomato sauce and flour into a mixing bowl or food processor. Add half of the lightly beaten egg (reserve the remaining egg to use as a glaze), then mix to combine.

Divide the filling into nine equal pieces, and roll these into balls. Brush the smaller square of pastry lightly with a little milk, mark it lightly into nine equal-sized squares (three rows of three) and arrange the balls of filling on these. Flatten each ball slightly, and sprinkle each with a little grated cheese.

Roll the other square of pastry loosely round the rolling pin (so it is not stretched), then lie it on top of the balls. Using the rolling pin and your fingers press the two layers of pastry together between and outside the mince mounds, then cut air vents in the top of each 'pie'.

Cut between the mounds with a knife or serrated cutting wheel, to give nine little parcels. Brush the nine square pieburgers with the reserved beaten egg. If desired, re-roll pastry "off cuts", then cut them into strips and decorate the glazed tops of the Pieburgers.

Lift onto an oven tray covered with baking paper or a Teflon liner. Sprinkle with lightly toasted sesame seeds if desired. Bake at 200°C for about 30 minutes or until golden brown. Reduce the temperature after 15–20 minutes if they brown too quickly.

Serve hot, warm, reheated or cold. Refrigerate up to 2 days or wrap individually and freeze up to 3 months.

Easy Pizza Base

Home-made yeasted pizza bases are hard to beat, and are really very easy to prepare, particularly if you have a breadmaker.

For 1 very large, 2 medium, or 8 individual bases:

3 tsp instant active dried yeast
½ cup milk
¾ cup boiling water
2 tsp sugar
1½ tsp salt
2 Tbsp olive or canola oil
3 cups high grade flour
additional flour or water if required

If making by hand: Measure the yeast into a large bowl. Combine the milk and water, and add this to the yeast along with the sugar, salt and oil. Leave to stand for a couple of minutes, then add half the flour and stir well to make a thick batter, then add the remaining flour and stir to make a dough firm enough to knead (add extra flour if required). Tip onto a floured surface and knead for 5–10 minutes, then cover the dough loosely and leave to rise for about 10 minutes before using.

If using a bread machine: Measure all the ingredients into the machine, set the machine to the "Dough" cycle and press start. Check the dough after a few minutes of mixing and if it looks too wet add a little extra flour, or a little water if too dry. The dough can be removed from the machine any time after about 30 minutes from the start of mixing, or, if you have time, let the cycle run through.

Turn dough onto a floured surface and divide as required then roll each piece into a thin (5–7mm thick) round shape.

Pizzas

Pizzas make an excellent easy lunch – equally enjoyable hot, cold or reheated. There are many different options but at their simplest, it is just a matter of tossing a few selected toppings (even a collection of leftovers from the fridge) onto a bought or home-made base, and baking!

For 2 large or 8 individual pizzas:

1 recipe bread base (see above)
½ cup tomato pizza topping*

Select 2–3 from fillings list
250–350g sliced, grated, or crumbled cheese (mild or tasty cheddar, mozzarella, feta, or a mixture).
Olive oil to drizzle (optional)

Preheat the oven to 200°C while you assemble your pizza/s. Place the bases on a lightly oiled (or teflon lined) oven slide or pizza tray. Start by spreading the base/s with a thin layer of tomato topping, then add your selection of the suggested toppings (2–3 are generally plenty).

A little thinly sliced onion
Thinly sliced red/green/yellow capsicums
Sliced mushrooms
Sliced or diced ham/bacon, salami, sliced cooked sausages, shredded chicken, assorted seafood or surimi, etc.
Thin slices or wedges of tomato (or halved cherry tomatoes)
Char-grilled or roasted vegetables (tomatoes, mushrooms, capsicums, eggplant, zucchini, artichoke hearts etc.)
Anchovies and/or chopped olives
Chopped fresh or dried basil, thyme etc.

Top with a generous layer of sliced, grated, or crumbled cheese, and if you like, drizzle lightly with olive oil.

Bake at 200°C for 10–15 minutes, or until the base has browned underneath.

*use a bought mixture, or stir together ½ cup tomato paste, 1 tsp garlic salt, ½ tsp basil or oregano and pepper to taste. Add 2–3 Tbsp water and mix to make an easily spreadable paste.

Calzone & Stromboli

If you do make your own pizza bases, why not try something a little different with these 'closed' pizzas – they're really well suited to being transported.

CALZONE: Arrange pizza fillings over one half of (individual-sized) base/s, leaving 2cm uncovered at the edge. Moisten round the edge, then fold the uncovered half over the filled half to make a half moon shape, pressing the edges together. Bake like a pizza.

STROMBOLI (Pictured on page 49)**:** Roll 1 recipe of the pizza base into 2 large (50 x 75cm), very thin rectangle/s. Top like pizza (use toppings sparingly) leaving a 5cm strip at one of the short edges uncovered. Brush the uncovered edge lightly with water, then starting at the other short edge, roll the dough up like a sponge roll.

Place the roll on a baking sheet so it sits seam-side down, then slash the top diagonally a couple of times to prevent splitting and bake as for pizza.

Pide (Turkish Pizza)

These boat-shaped little pies are the Turkish equivalent of pizza.

For 4 'pide' (4–6 servings):

1 pizza dough recipe (see page 48)

1 Tbsp olive or canola oil
1 medium onion, diced
500g minced lamb
¼ cup currants
1 tsp paprika
½ tsp mint
½ tsp cinnamon
¼ tsp chilli powder, optional
½ tsp salt
2 cups (200g) grated cheddar or crumbled feta cheese
4 eggs

Preheat the oven to 200°C.

Working on a lightly floured surface, divide the pizza dough into four equal portions. Shape each portion into a ball, then roll each ball into an oval about 30cm long and 20cm wide. Place the ovals on non-stick sprayed or lightly oiled baking sheets (you should be able to get two per sheet), brush the outer edge of each oval with water and fold in 1–2cm of the dough to form a canoe or eye shape. Leave the dough to rise at room temperature while you prepare the filling.

Heat the oil in a large pan. Add the onion and cook for 3–4 minutes, stirring occasionally, until the onion is soft, then add the mince. Cook, stirring frequently to break up any lumps, for about 5 minutes longer, until the lamb is lightly browned. Stir in the next six ingredients and cook for a couple of minutes longer before removing from the heat.

Spread a quarter of the lamb mixture over each of the bases (leaving the folded edge clear), then sprinkle them evenly with the grated (or crumbled) cheese. Break one of the eggs into a small bowl, whisk it with a fork, then pour the egg evenly over the filling of one pide. Repeat this process until all four are egg-covered.

Place two racks near the middle of the oven, slide in the trays of pide and bake for 12–15 minutes (swap the trays over after about 6 minutes), until the bottoms are lightly browned.

Serve with a simple green or tomato salad.

Spinach & Feta Pies

These very simple little pies are loosely based on Greek Spanakopita – they look great for a minimum of effort. They can be served hot, warm or cold so really are versatile.

For 8–10 packages:
1 Tbsp olive oil
1 medium onion, diced
¼ cup pine nuts (optional)
200–250g frozen spinach,
 thawed and drained
100–150g feta cheese,
 crumbled
¼ tsp dried basil
¼ tsp thyme
¼ tsp freshly grated
 nutmeg
¼–½ tsp salt
black pepper to taste
1 large egg
8–10 sheets filo pastry
about 2 Tbsp melted butter
 or olive oil

Preheat the oven to 200°C.

Heat the oil in a medium-sized frypan, add the onion and cook until softened. Stir in the pine nuts (if using) and continue to cook until these are golden brown.

While the onion cooks, squeeze as much liquid as you can from the thawed spinach. Place the spinach in a large bowl and add the crumbled cheese, then the seasonings and the onion-pine nut mixture. (The quantity of salt required will depend on the saltiness of the feta – vary it to taste.) Add the egg and stir until well mixed.

Lay one sheet of filo on a dry surface and brush it lightly with oil, then fold it lengthways to make a long, narrow rectangle. Place about ¼ cup of the filling mixture (don't be too generous) close to one end of the strip, then fold the corner up diagonally to cover the filling (so the bottom edge meets the side). Keep folding the filling (straight then diagonally) until you reach the end of the strip. Fold any extra pastry under the package, brush lightly with oil or melted butter and place on a baking tray. Repeat until all the filling is used.

Bake for 10–12 minutes until golden brown and firm when pressed gently in the centre. Serve hot, warm or even cold.

Sushi

A platter or box of several different shapes and varieties of sushi makes a tasty and interesting meal.

For 2–3 main servings:
1 cup short-grain or sushi
rice
1¾ cups boiling water
2 Tbsp rice or wine vinegar
2 Tbsp sugar
1 Tbsp sherry
1 tsp salt

Place the rice in a large container and cover with cold water. Drain the rice, then cover with water and drain again.

To microwave: Put the rice in a large microwave bowl. Add the boiling water then cover the bowl and microwave at Medium (50%) power for 15–20 minutes or until the rice is completely tender. Remove the bowl from the microwave and stir in the vinegar, sugar, sherry and salt. Leave rice to cool to room temperature.

To cook conventionally: Put the rice in a large heavy pot (with a close-fitting lid), pour in the boiling water, bring rice to the boil, then cover pot and reduce the heat to very low and leave to steam for 15 minutes. Remove the pot from the heat and stand for a further 10 minutes before stirring in the vinegar, sugar, sherry and salt. Leave rice to cool to room temperature.

The fillings you choose will depend on the type of sushi you are making and your own preferences, but here are a few suggestions:

Filling suggestions:
strips of cucumber
strips of carrot
sliced avocado
strips of red/green/yellow
capsicum
smoked (or raw) salmon
strips of omelette
shredded surimi
fresh (or canned) tuna
pickled ginger
pickled vegetables
wasabi paste
yaki nori (roasted seaweed
sheets)

Rolled Sushi (Maki-sushi)

Sushi rolls are actually very easy to make. Lay a sheet of nori on a clean dry bench or sushi mat (the mat makes getting the roll started a little easier). Spread a layer of rice about 1cm thick over the nori, leaving a 2–3cm strip down one long edge clear. Arrange selected filling/s along the middle of the rice. Brush the exposed nori with a little water, then roll up starting from the rice-covered edge. Sit the roll seam side down for 2–3 minutes before cutting into 2–3cm thick slices with a sharp (wet) knife.

Hand Rolls (Temaki-sushi)

Cut a sheet of nori in half lengthwise. Place one strip on the bench and spread a heaped tablespoon of rice diagonally across one end. Arrange a few strips of your selected filling on top of the rice. Fold the exposed corner across the filling, then roll the sheet up to form a cone.

Moulded Sushi (Nigiri-sushi)

Press a heaped tablespoon of rice into the moistened palm of one hand. Squeeze and shape the rice until it is flat on the bottom and curved on the top (adjust the size to suit the size of the fish you will use). Spread one side of a thinly sliced piece of raw (or cold smoked) salmon or tuna with wasabi, then place it wasabi side down over the curved side of the rice. Decorate with a thin 'belt' of nori if desired.

To serve: Arrange your sushi on plates or a platter and serve with pickled ginger, wasabi paste and a bowl of Kikkoman soy sauce for dipping.

Marvellous Muffins
(Sweet & Savoury)

Muffins are more-ish! Easy to make, not too rich and fine to make ahead and freeze, a muffin is a great addition to any lunchbox, or the perfect accompaniment to a cup of tea or coffee at any time.

Blueberry Bran Muffins

Here is our version of a classic American favourite. Make a batch and freeze them in ones or twos to grab out of the freezer for a perfect lunch or snack on the run.

For 12–15 regular-sized muffins:

1 cup baking bran (wheat bran)
¼ cup wheatgerm or extra bran
½ cup canola oil
1 cup plain or fruity yoghurt
1 large egg
¾ cup wholemeal flour
¾ cup high grade (bread) flour
1 tsp cinnamon
1 tsp baking powder
¾ tsp salt
½ tsp baking soda
1 cup brown sugar
1–1½ cups (150–180g) frozen blueberries

Preheat the oven to 200°C (190°C fanbake), with the rack just below the middle.

Measure the first five ingredients into a large bowl, mix to blend everything with a fork, then leave to stand. (If you don't have wheatgerm in the house, replace it with extra bran.)

Measure the remaining dry ingredients into a medium-sized bowl, and stir well with a fork to mix thoroughly. Do not thaw the blueberries, but separate any clumps of berries. (We use half a 350g packet and find that this is a very good amount for this recipe, although you can use less.)

Tip the flour mixture into the liquid mixture, then fold everything together until the dry ingredients are moistened.

Spoon the mixture into 12–15 medium or about 30 mini muffin pans which have been thoroughly non-stick sprayed.

Bake for about 15 minutes (longer than most other muffins, because of the frozen berries in the mixture) until centres spring back when pressed. Remove from the oven and leave to cool for several minutes before removing from the pans.

Serve warm or cool completely on racks then freeze in airtight bags – grab a couple from the freezer on the way out the door in the morning, add a piece of fruit and you've got lunch sorted!

Triple Chocolate & Banana Muffins

With cocoa, and light AND dark choc bits, these muffins are bound to be popular, and they're simple to make!

For 12–15 regular-sized muffins:

2–3 medium bananas, mashed (1 cup total)
1 large egg
½ cup canola or other light vegetable oil
½ cup milk
¼ tsp salt
¾ cup sugar
¼ cup dark (or milk) chocolate bits
¼ cup white chocolate bits
¼ cup cocoa powder
2 cups self-raising flour

Preheat oven to 200°C (or 190°C fanbake).

Mash the ripe bananas on a board, using a fork, then place in a large bowl. Add the egg, oil, milk, salt and sugar then mix together well. Sprinkle in the chocolate bits and cocoa powder and stir until evenly mixed.

Stir the flour in its container, then spoon it into the cup measure without packing it or banging it down. Sprinkle it over the top of the other ingredients then fold it in without over-mixing, stopping when there are no streaks or pockets of flour visible.

Spoon into the mini-muffin pans or regular muffin pans which have been thoroughly sprayed with non-stick spray. Bake for 12–15 minutes or until the tops spring back when pressed lightly (cooking time does vary from oven to oven and with the size of the muffins). Leave to stand 2–3 minutes in their pans, then remove carefully and cool on a rack.

When completely cooled, store in an airtight container or pack into plastic bags and freeze for longer term storage.

Easy Cheesy Muffins

Some years ago, during a bakers' strike, an easy bread made from self-raising flour and beer "did the rounds". Starting with the same basic ingredients, you can make wonderful cheesy muffins!

For 12 generous medium-sized muffins or 24 mini muffins:

2 cups standard (plain) flour
2 cups (200g) grated tasty cheese
1 large egg
1 cup lager or beer
about 2 Tbsp chutney or Thai sweet chilli sauce (optional)

Preheat the oven to 220°C (210°C fanbake), with the rack just below the middle.

Toss the flour and grated cheese together in a large bowl.

Break the egg into another large bowl and beat with a fork enough to thoroughly mix the white and yolk. Add the lager or beer (which can be flat or bubbly) and stir to mix briefly, then sprinkle in the flour and cheese mixture.

Fold together until most of the flour is dampened, but do not overmix. If you like the idea, drizzle your favourite chutney or sweet chilli sauce over the surface, and fold it in lightly so that it stays in streaks.

Spoon the mixture into 12 non-stick sprayed medium muffin pans. Bake for 10-15 minutes, until the muffins are nicely browned and the centres spring back when pressed. Stand for 2–3 minutes before removing from the pans.

Warm or cold, cheese muffins are always a very popular lunch. Warm mini-muffins make excellent party snacks.

VARIATIONS: Try adding 50g of chopped ham or salami and/or a finely chopped spring onion to the mixture.

Spinach & Feta Muffins

Spinach and feta cheese is a combination that always seems to work well, and these are no exception! The green flecks from the spinach make these muffins look really good too.

For 12 regular muffins:

½ cup (100–125g) cooked spinach, chopped*
1 cup milk
1 cup (250g) cottage cheese
¼ cup canola oil
1 large egg
75g–100g feta, cubed or crumbled
1 cup wholemeal flour
1 cup plain flour
4 tsp baking powder
½–1 tsp salt

* For convenience try using ½ a 250g block of frozen spinach.

Preheat oven to 210°C (200°C fanbake), with the rack just below the middle.

Lightly squeeze the cooked spinach, reserving the liquid. Make the spinach liquid up to 1 cup with milk, then place the spinach, milk, cottage cheese, oil and egg in a large bowl and mix well. Add the cubed or crumbled cheese and mix lightly.

Measure the flours, baking powder and salt together into another bowl and toss together with a whisk or fork.

Tip the flour mixture into the liquids, then fold gently together until the flour is just moistened. The mixture does not need to be smooth.

Spoon the mixture into 12 non-stick sprayed regular muffin pans, then bake at 210°C (200°C fanbake) for 15 minutes or until golden brown and a skewer poked into the centre of a muffin comes out clean.

Remove muffins from the oven and leave to cool in their pans for 2–3 minutes (this helps reduce sticking) before tipping out and cooling on a rack.

Delicious warm, or store cooled muffins in sealed bags to prevent drying out. Freeze for longer term storage.

Sweet Treats

(Biscuits, Bars & Slices)

We hope you'll try our "sweet treats", and find that they delight you, your friends and family! This selection of goodies aren't hard to make and most of them have some "good for you" properties. Tuck one or two into your pocket, purse, briefcase or pack to make any lunch seem complete.

Pack-A-Snack Bar

This bar makes a popular, concentrated snack food. With its many nutritious additions, it is almost a meal in itself, and it is solid enough to travel well in a lunchbox, sports bag, briefcase or handbag.

For an 18x28cm slice, about 12 servings:

Base:

1 cup standard (plain) flour
1 cup wholemeal flour
1 cup Instant Oats
200g chilled butter
1 cup brown sugar

Topping:

4 large eggs
½ cup brown sugar
1 tsp vanilla essence
2 cups almonds
1 cup dates, chopped
1 cup dried apricots, chopped
1 cup chocolate bits or melts
1 cup desiccated coconut

Preheat oven to 180°C (170°C fanbake), with the rack just below the middle of the oven. Line the sides and bottom of a pan about 18x28cm with baking paper.

For base, chop the flours, oats and cubed butter together in a food processor (or grate the butter into the oats and flours in a bowl), then mix in the brown sugar and press the mixture into the prepared pan.

For topping, put eggs, brown sugar and vanilla in a large bowl and beat with a fork just until whites and yolks are evenly mixed. Add all the remaining ingredients and mix together with a stirrer or spatula. Spread over the uncooked base and press down fairly evenly.

Bake for 45 minutes, covering the top with a Teflon liner or folded baking paper part way through the cooking if it browns too quickly. Leave to cool in the baking pan, preferably overnight.

When completely cold, cut into four large pieces using a sharp serrated knife. Trim off the outer edges if necessary, then cut the large bars into three smaller bars or fingers.

Store pieces in the refrigerator up to a week, or freeze for up to six weeks in plastic bags or covered containers.

Chewy 'Muesli' Slice

The addition of crushed weetbix and plenty of dried fruit gives this interesting slice a 'healthy feel'. It is solid enough to travel well and makes a nice addition to a lunch or is a great pre- or post game or training snack.

For an 18x28cm slice, 12–16 servings:

125g butter
2 household tablespoons golden syrup
1 cup lightly packed brown sugar
1 tsp vanilla
1 large egg
1 cup standard (plain) flour
1 tsp baking powder
6 weetbix, crushed
1 cup coconut thread
1½ cups dried fruit (we like sultanas or raisins, chopped dried apricots and dried cranberries)
½ cup chocolate bits or chips

Preheat oven to 180°C.

Measure the butter, golden syrup and sugar into a large pot or microwave bowl and heat until the butter has melted (about 1 minute on High (100%) power). Stir to combine, then add the vanilla and egg and mix again.

Sift in the flour and baking powder, then add the remaining ingredients and stir until evenly combined.

Line an 18X28cm tin with baking paper or a Teflon liner, then press the mixture evenly into this. Bake for 20–30 minutes or until the top is golden brown and the centre feels about as firm as the edges (reduce the heat a little if the top browns too fast).

Remove from the oven and cool in the tin for 5–10 minutes before removing from the pan and cooling completely on a rack. Cut into the desired sized pieces using a sharp knife, and store in an airtight container until required.

Giant Peanut Butter & Chocolate Cookies

These are a variant of a delicious American cookie recipe, and are slightly chewy rather than crisp when cooked. Their larger size means they make a substantial snack or addition to a packed lunch, rather than just being a little extra something on the side.

For about 12 giant cookies:

100g butter, softened
¾ cup crunchy peanut butter
1 cup brown sugar
1 egg
1 tsp vanilla essence
2 Tbsp golden syrup
1½ cups flour
1 tsp baking soda
½ cup chocolate bits or chips

24 squares of chocolate to decorate (optional)

Preheat the oven to 190°C (or 180°C for fanbake).

Beat the butter and peanut butter together in a large bowl. Add the sugar, egg, vanilla and golden syrup then beat until fluffy. Sift in the flour and baking soda and sprinkle in the chocolate pieces, then stir to combine.

Scoop ¼ cup measures of the mixture onto a baking paper or Teflon lined baking sheet leaving some room for spreading, flatten them out to about 10cm across with the palm of your hand.

Bake for 10–12 minutes until just beginning to brown, then place 2 squares of chocolate on top of each biscuit (if using) and bake for another 2–3 minutes. Remove from the oven and cool on the tray for 5 minutes, then transfer to a wire rack.

Store in an airtight container until required.

Easy Oaty Cookies

This recipe makes a generous batch of delicious biscuits – a few added to a packed lunch will brighten anyone's day! The sultanas, nuts and seeds are not an absolute requirement, but the inclusion of one, two or all of them does add interest.

For about 60 biscuits, depending on size:

200g butter
1 cup packed brown sugar
1 cup white sugar
1 large egg
¼ cup milk
½ tsp baking soda
1 tsp vanilla essence
1 cup standard (plain) flour
3 cups (instant) rolled oats
½ cup sultanas (optional)
½ cup chopped walnuts (optional)
½ cup sunflower seeds (optional)

Preheat oven to 180°C (170°C fanbake), with the rack just below the middle. Line a baking tray with baking paper or a Teflon liner.

Melt the butter in a large pot or microwaveable bowl, removing from the heat as soon as it is liquid. Stir in the sugars and egg. Mix the milk, soda and vanilla together and add to the mixture. Sprinkle the flour, rolled oats (and any optional ingredients), over everything else and mix until well combined. Drop mixture in teaspoon lots onto the prepared baking tray, leaving room for spreading.

Bake for 10–12 minutes, or until biscuits are golden brown and feel firm. (Shape the next tray of biscuits while this one cooks.) While biscuits are warm, lift them onto a cooling rack. (If they cool too much and are hard to lift off, put the tray back in the oven for about a minute.) Store in airtight containers once cold.

Index

Knives etc., by Mail Order

For about 20 years I have imported my favourite, very sharp kitchen knives from Switzerland. They keep their edges well, are easy to sharpen, a pleasure to use, and make excellent gifts.

VEGETABLE KNIFE $8.00
Ideal for cutting and peeling vegetables, these knives have a straight edged 85mm blade and black (dishwasher-proof) nylon handle. Each knife comes in an individual plastic sheath.

BONING/UTILITY KNIFE $9.50
Excellent for boning chicken and other meats, and/or for general kitchen duties. Featuring a 103mm blade that curves to a point and a dishwasher-proof, black nylon handle. Each knife comes in a plastic sheath.

SERRATED KNIFE $9.50
These knives are unbelievably useful. They are perfect for cutting cooked meats, ripe fruit and vegetables, and slicing bread and baking. Treated carefully, these blades stay sharp for years. The serrated 110mm blade is rounded at the end with a black (dishwasher-proof) nylon handle and each knife comes in an individual plastic sheath.

THREE-PIECE SET $22.00
This three-piece set includes a vegetable knife, a serrated knife (as described above) and a right-handed potato peeler with a matching black handle, presented in a white plastic wallet.

GIFT BOXED KNIFE SET $44.00
This set contains five knives plus a matching right-handed potato peeler. There is a straight bladed vegetable knife and a serrated knife (as above), as well as a handy 85mm serrated blade vegetable knife, a small (85mm) utility knife with a pointed tip and a smaller (85mm) serrated knife. These elegantly presented sets make ideal gifts.

SERRATED CARVING KNIFE $28.50
This fabulous knife cuts beautifully and is a pleasure to use, it's ideal for carving or cutting fresh bread. The 21cm serrated blade does not require sharpening. Once again the knife has a black moulded, dishwasher safe handle and comes in a plastic sheath.

COOK'S KNIFE $35.00
An excellent all-purpose kitchen knife. With a well balanced 19cm wedge-shaped blade and a contoured black nylon handle, these knives make short work of slicing and chopping, and have come out on top of their class in several comparative tests. Each dishwasher-safe knife comes with its own plastic sheath.

STEEL $20.00
These steels have a 20cm 'blade' and measure 33cm in total. With its matching black handle the steel is an ideal companion for your own knives, or as a gift. Alison gets excellent results using these steels. N.B. Not for use with serrated knives.

PROBUS SPREADER/SCRAPER $7.50
After her knives, these are the most used tools in Alison's kitchen! With a comfortable plastic handle, metal shank and flexible plastic blade (suitable for use on non-stick surfaces), these are excellent for mixing muffin batters, stirring and scraping bowls, spreading icings, turning pikelets etc., etc....

ACCUTECH 'DUAL' GRATER $26.00
This indispensable kitchen tool, a relatively new invention, is the length and width of a ruler, and is two graters in one – fine at one end and coarser at the other! Use the fine end for citrus peel, nutmeg, garlic, ginger, parmesan, and the coarse end for chocolate, cheese, carrot, garlic, ginger etc. Razor-sharp, easy to use, and at a friendly price to boot, this fantastic microplane-like grater is an asset in any kitchen!

NON-STICK TEFLON LINERS
Re-usable SureBrand Teflon liners are another essential kitchen item – they really help avoid the frustration of stuck-on baking, roasting or frying. Once you've used them, you'll wonder how you did without!

Round tin liner	
(for 15-23cm tins)	$6.50
(for 23-30cm tins)	$9.50
Square tin liner	
(for 15-23cm tins)	$6.50
(for 23-30cm tins)	$9.50
Ring tin liner	
(for 23cm tins)	$6.95
Baking sheet liner	
(33x44cm)	$13.95

All prices include GST. Prices current at time of publishing, subject to change without notice. Please add $3.50 post & packing to all orders (any number of items).

Make cheques payable to Alison Holst Mail Orders and post to: **Alison Holst Mail Orders**
FREEPOST 124807
PO Box 17016
Wellington

Or visit us at **www.holst.co.nz**